inside China

inside China

◻ NATIONAL GEOGRAPHIC

Washington, D.C.

CONTENTS

SEBASTIAO SALGADO
Preceding Pages
Workers in a café in the city's center
SHANGHAI, 1998

ANIU
Opposite
A well-dressed Pekingese
SHENZHEN, GUANGDONG PROVINCE,
2001

CHARLES OMMANNEY
A farmer takes his goods to market in the early morning.
PINGYAO, SHANXI PROVINCE, 2006

6

MERL LA VOY

Mrs. Chiang Kai-shek
KIANGSU, SHANGHAI, 1933

8

MARK HENLEY

**A training session at the Shaolin
martial arts school**
HENAN PROVINCE, 2004

RAYMOND GEHMAN

**Construction on a domed
swimming pool**
QINHUANGDAS, HEBEI PROVINCE, 1999

DAVID BUTOW

Girls work in a sweet shop in Shanghai's Old Town.
SHANGHAI, 2006

INTRODUCTION

HOW DOES ONE GET INSIDE CHINA? Or, to put it another way, how do we know when we have arrived there? History used to help, and so did a knowledge of geography. But now the geographic certainties are vanishing in the face of the sheer vastness of the projects that are under way: In today's China, railways traverse and pierce through some of the world's highest terrain as they drive their way to Tibet; the gorges of the mid-Yangtze River, once staples of art, setters of standards in verse, their shores worn by the feet of uncountable trackers, are vanishing before our eyes; the paddy fields and the orchards disappear under the weight of the concrete poured over them to support the new high-rise cities, the highways, the airfields. Where is it now, this place, this Hong Kong, this Anhui, this Shenyang, this Shanghai? Where are our anchors and our gazetteers? Where can we plant our feet or fasten our minds with any sense of certainty?

As for history, that once familiar guide, the Chinese communist leadership sees little need to explain or investigate itself, while we in the West are instructed by our peers to shun all "master narratives," so that our tales become leaderless, and our ability to dig deeper falters. Who are these families, gazing carefully at us, in black and white, so neatly dressed, so calm and poised, so ready—apparently—to take charge? Why are all those children starving in what-ever town they have tumbled into? Who are these girls, arms akimbo, marching in rows to the beat of a music that we cannot hear?

One of the delights of China, to many generations of Western observers, was its apparent accessibility despite its enormous size, the fact that it seemed governed by clear rules and regulations, that rulers and subordinates all had their places, that the country had somehow developed

International boundary
Provincial boundary
Disputed boundary
Great Wall
⊛ Capital
● ● ● Selected populated place

Geographic Terms
Pendi .... Basin
S.A.R. .... Special Administrative Region
Shamo .... Desert
Shan .... Mountain-s

0   100   200   300   400
kilometers

0   100   200   300   400
statute miles

RUSSIA

KAZAKHSTAN

KYRGYZSTAN

TAJIKISTAN

AFGHAN.

PAKISTAN

INDIA

ALTAY MOUNTAINS

•Ürümqi
•Turpan

TIAN SHAN

XINJIANG UYGUR

TARIM PENDI
Taklimakan Shamo

K U N L U N   S H A N

Gasherbrum II
+ 8,035 m

Boundary
claimed
by India

Boundary
claimed
by China

PLATEAU OF TIBET

XIZANG
(TIBET)

•Lhasa

Mount Everest
(Qomolangma)
+ 29,035 m

Yarlung Zangbo
(Brahmaputra)

NEPAL

BHUTAN

Boundary
claimed by China

INDIA

BANGLADESH

Yulongxue Shan
+ 5,596 m

MYANMAR
(BURMA)

•Dali
•Baoshan

YUNNAN

Dian
Chi

•Kunming

LAOS

MONGOLIA

G O B I

GANSU

•Wuwei

QINGHAI

•Xining
Kulun
Shankou   •Tongren

Huang
(Yellow)

C H I N A

•Lanzhou

NINGXIA

Yan'an•

SHAANXI

•Xi'an

SICHUAN

•Chengdu

•Chongqing
•Fengdu

Jinsha (Yangtze)

Nu (Salween)

Lancang (Mekong)

Lancang
(Mekong)

Gulf of
Tonkin

VIETNAM

HAINAN

GUIZHOU

•Leishan
•Rongjiang

GUANGXI

•Yangshuo

•Guilin

Three
Gorges
Dam

CHONGQING

HUBEI

•Wuhan

•Hankou

Dongting
Hu

•Liuyang

HUNAN

JIANGXI

GUANGDONG

Zhu (Pearl)

Guangzhou•
(Canton)
Panyu•
Macau•

Dongguan•
Shenzhen•
Jiulong (Kowloon)•
•Hong Kong

HONG KONG (XIANGGANG), S.A.R.

MACAU
(AOMEN),
S.A.R.

•Shantou
(Swatow)

FUJIAN

•Quanzhou

•Xiamen
(Amoy)

SOUTH CHINA SEA

PHILIPPINES

RUSSIA

MANCHURIA

HEILONGJIANG

•Harbin Songhua
•Acheng

•Changchun   Songhua

JILIN

•Baotou
•Datong
Pianguan•

Beijing
(Peking) ⊛

HEBEI

•Gaoyang

•Taiyuan
SHANXI
Pingyao•
•Panlong

Fen

Huang (Yellow)

•Zhengzhou
(Chengchow)

HENAN

•Songxian   •Huaiyang
Bengbu•
Fengyang•
Hefei•

ANHUI

Tianjin•
(Tientsin)

Wuqiao•

SHANDONG
•Laiwu

Shenyang•
LIAONING   •Benxi
Anshan• •Liaoyang

NORTH
KOREA

Qinhuangdao•
•Dalian
(Dairen)

Bo Hai

YELLOW
SEA

SOUTH
KOREA

JAPAN

Yu

JIANGSU

Zhenjiang• •Yangzhou
Nanjing•
Songjiang•
Haining•

•Suzhoa   •Shanghai
SHANGHAI SHI

Hangzhou• •Ningbo
Xianju•

ZHEJIANG

•Wenzhou

Siming
Mts.

EAST
CHINA
SEA

Taiwan Strait

TAIWAN

Huai

Chang Jiang (Yangtze)

TAIWAN
The People's Republic of China claims
Taiwan as its 23rd province. Taiwan's
government (Republic of China) maintains
that there are two political entities.

17

into a harmonious synthesis. Even as they knew they would never be able to see it all, the observers felt they had seen enough to understand it, and that nothing need be left unsaid. So they could isolate certain pieces of the puzzle, interpret them as they chose, and fill in any gaps from their imaginations. Now, moving toward the end of the 21st century's first decade, China is accessible to foreign would-be viewers to an unprecedented extent. But the sheer amount of choices we are now offered is baffling, and thus the temptation is to make our decisions at random, relying on juxtapositions and paradoxes to tell the story: the skyscraper and the trash heap, the hooker and the temple, the lattice window frame and the bulldozer, the dance lessons in the dark.

In his witty novel *Citizen of the World*, written in the mid-18th century, the Irish writer Oliver Goldsmith has a fictional Chinese visitor to London tell his friend back home that pretentious English pedagogues "almost reasoned me out of my country." It is a wonderful way to summarize the self-absorbed thinking of what we call the "Enlightenment," but in our present age we need to face another side of that aphorism: We have to try and comprehend how the Chinese seem to be reasoning themselves out of their own history and culture, their own traditions, their own sense of order.

To a dedicated China watcher like myself, the pictures collected in this volume constitute a wondrous mixture of the familiar and the strange. A few have become icons for a forgotten time; most are strikingly new, sometimes shocking in their honesty and unexpectedness. Cumulatively, what we are offered here is disturbing, but disturbing in a positive sense: It jolts us out of our complacency, reveals the gaps in our understanding, challenges clichés, pushes us to disentangle the truly elegant from the crass, the surface texture from the deeper message.

These photographs, though often seeming to be so inconceivably different from each other, all have one thing in common that gives them a kind of unity. They each represent a moment in the poignant and often agonizing march into the wider world that China has been taking over the past century. That march spans the period from the last years of the Qing dynasty's Empress Dowager Cixi (who died in 1908) to the upcoming extravaganza of the 2008 Olympic games. This century-long march has led China and the Chinese through the experience of almost every kind of human polity: a popularly elected parliament, an imperial restoration, the unpredictable hazards of warlordism, the rise of a single-party nationalist state, the humiliations and the horrors of the protracted Japanese invasion, an internecine civil war, and the emergence of a new single-party state (this time a Marxist-Leninist one) in 1949. That state, in its turn, has moved from a Stalinist model of rigid central control over agriculture, industry, and culture, through an extremist period of revolutionary experiments with enforced collectivization, to the wild and destructive internal strife of the Cultural Revolution, and on to the initially unplanned and still evolving helter-skelter tumble into the post-Maoist world of "capitalism with socialist characteristics," presided over—with different degrees of effectiveness—by Deng Xiaoping and his successors.

It is not surprising, after this century of turmoil, that China can still seem so unsure of itself. The new prosperity experienced by many millions is firmly enmeshed with the new-found poverty of millions more. The armies of stock market speculators with their mobile phones and sleek automobiles are matched by the armies of the migrant workers in their shantytowns. Vibrant cities are emerging from once fertile farmland, and have proved voracious in their demands for ever more space, and reckless in their consumption of scarce resources of fuel and water. The Chinese government, building its claims on its (only vaguely defined) communist roots, struggles ineffectively to keep some control over the deteriorating environment with its falling water tables, chemically polluted streams, acid rain, and eroded hills. The so-called minority peoples on China's peripheries are dressed up in their once special clothes to serve as entertainment for the newly prosperous Chinese tourists. An unsorted tangle of Western fashions fills storefront windows, Chinese popular music struggles to find its own voice, "Miss Lonelyhearts" advisors steel the faint-hearted on their radio shows, and billboards and TV advertisements seek to form a profitable consumer consensus.

All of this—and so much more—is inside China. Where it will lead is impossible to say. But that this is, and will remain, an exciting and varied journey is richly documented by the photographs presented here. It is not surprising that there is no obvious unity binding all these images together: We are still far too near the beginnings of this particular story either to expect, or to want, that this should be so. ■

china: Landscape

Landscape: Our first image of China is often that immortalized by traditional Chinese painting or poetry: the mist-shrouded, craggy peaks of Mount Huangshan in southeast China, or the spectacular lakes and waterfalls of Jiuzhaigou in southwest China. The arid mountains and desert landscape of China's northwest, where camels still traverse, offer another sense of China's land, one that can transport us back in time to the days of the Silk Road. And the Great Wall, labored over by 400,000 Chinese, carved into the sides of mountains, stacked across the desert, and spanning almost 4,000 miles across Northern China, remains the most famous, dramatic symbol of China today.

A second look brings us a startlingly different landscape. Gleaming cities filled with candy-colored skyscrapers dominate the skyline of the country's eastern seaboard, paying tribute to the rising prosperity of the country. New monuments to China's glory such as the Olympic Stadium sprout from the ground; grand-scale infrastructure projects, in the tradition of the Three Gorges Dam, transform the country's geography; and across the country, hundreds of thousands of factories dot the land, fueling China's rising economic power, while challenging the ability of the land, water, and air to sustain such growth.

Yet these pictures provide only a snapshot of this vast complex country, its history, peoples, and cultures. China's land and the ways in which it has been, and continues to be, transformed can provide a much deeper understanding of the country's broader social trends and epic events. The interaction between the country's people and its environment illuminates not only a rich and tumultuous history but also a vibrant—sometimes chaotic—present, as well as a challenging future.

Roughly the same size as the United States, China is a spectacularly geographically diverse country with temperatures that range from arctic to tropical. The Tibetan plateau in China's southwest sits more than 13,000 feet above sea level, and its glaciers provide water for two of the world's ten longest rivers, the Yangtze and the Yellow. Throughout China's central and southern region in provinces such as Yunnan and Sichuan provinces, the mostly green landscape is rich in forests and punctuated by dramatic mountain gorges, waterfalls, and rivers. China's northern plains present a dramatically different landscape: water scarce, with grasslands and a vast and expanding desert. Low hills and broad plains define much of the densely populated central and coastal China, and support the richest agriculture and thriving industry of the country.

Yet even this description captures only a moment in time. China's geography is constantly evolving—sometimes in barely perceptible ways and sometimes with great drama. Through the centuries, the Chinese people have exerted a profound impact on their land, transforming the geography from one rich in forested land to one in which less than 20 percent of the land boasts forest cover. Seven mighty river systems, two of which, the Yellow and the Yangtze, wend their way virtually across the entire expanse of the country have traditionally provided ample water to sustain the Chinese people and their land. Today, the people can no longer rely on the Yellow River to reach the ocean, and vast areas of the country are water scarce. China's land, too, once heralded by ancient scribes for its fertile soil, is now one-quarter desert, producing tens if not hundreds of thousands of environmental migrants annually.

To understand the transformation of China's land is to understand a history of devastating wars, efforts to consolidate territory, burgeoning population pressures, and relentless drives to develop the economy. China's land became an unwilling participant in a continuous cycle of economic development, environmental degradation, social dislocation, turmoil, and often violent political change.

As early as the establishment of China's first centralized state, the Qin Dynasty in 221 B.C., the country's rulers depended on and transformed the land in an effort to consolidate their power, feed their people, and develop their economy. In wartime, hillsides and grasslands were ravaged in the search for ores to make spears, cannons, and armor. In peacetime, forests were denuded and wetlands reclaimed for agriculture. The search for food to sustain a large and growing population—by the late 1600s, China had 100 million people—coupled with poor agricultural practices led to severe land degradation and deforestation. Farmers left rich soil infertile and moved on to deforest new areas, in the process contributing to both devastating floods and desertification. The Yellow River overflowed its banks once every two years in the Ming Dynasty (1368–1644) and almost once every year during the Qing Dynasty (1644–1912)—fulfilling its reputation as "China's Sorrow." At the same time, by the 1700s, vast areas in China's North and Northwest were submerged by sands, and the desert had begun its relentless expansion eastward.

In the 1900s, the fall of imperial China and the eventual rise of China's communists to power provided new impetus to transform the geography of the country. Mao Zedong, China's preeminent leader throughout the 1950s through early 1970s, launched what the historian Rhoads Murphey aptly termed at the time, "a war against nature." In an effort to catapult China's economy past that of the capitalist West, Mao pushed the country's farmers to achieve epic grain yields employing questionable agricultural practices. This "Great Leap Forward" campaign laid waste to forests and wetlands throughout the country and brought about a famine that left tens of millions of Chinese dead.

China's leaders also initiated a "third front" policy in an effort to defend against an invasion from the West that never came. They moved strategic heavy industries into the country's interior, thereby degrading and polluting the country's previously pristine natural habitats.

At the same time, Mao called on the Chinese people to set up smelters and create steel in backyard furnaces. By one estimate, 10 percent of China's forests were cut down to fire these furnaces. During this time, pollution also skyrocketed, and China's first minister of the environment, Qu Geping, reported that Beijing was transformed from a city that "did not produce even pencils" to one that boasted "700 factories and 2,000 blast furnaces belching soot in the air."

Today, China's geography is undergoing yet another profound transformation. Everywhere throughout the country, hills are being leveled, rivers rerouted, and dams constructed to meet the needs of an urbanization process that will revolutionize Chinese society in the coming decades. During the years

2000–2020, China's leaders anticipate relocating 300 million Chinese—roughly the entire population of the United States—to urban centers. New cities, covered in cranes and the dust of construction, are exploding with skyscrapers, European boutiques, and American fast food restaurants. Suburbs sprawl out with large homes in gated communities, private lakes, and golf courses.

China's leaders are also transforming the geography of the country in an effort to forge new economic and political linkages among the country's disparate and often competitive provinces. More than 52,000 miles of paved road are being laid to connect even the most remote regions of the country. These roads crisscross east and west, south and north, leaving the indelible imprint of development on China's land.

A series of further large-scale infrastructure projects promise to redraw the geographic and economic boundaries of the country. The Three Gorges Dam on the great Yangtze River—a monumental tribute to the vision of generations of Chinese leaders beginning with Sun Yat-sen—is located in China's Southwest, yet provides energy as far east as Shanghai. Similar hydropower projects in Yunnan Province provide energy thousands of miles away for Guangzhou's booming economy.

In addition, the just completed Qinghai-Tibetan railway that divides plateaus and burrows through mountains reflects as much a desire to enhance commerce and tourism in China's poorer western region as to link the perpetually politically problematic Tibet more concretely and inextricably to the government in Beijing.

And China's most recent grand-scale feat of engineering and hubris that will reconfigure the country's geography is the South to North China Water diversion project. This project, which will take decades to complete, will divert water from along the Yangtze River north to Beijing, Tianjin, and Hebei via three grand canals. Together, these canals will carry 44 billion m3—more than twice the volume of water that flows through the Colorado River—from points along the Yangtze to the parched northern provinces.

Such reengineering of China's land is not without cost. Towns and villages throughout the country are being razed to make room for modernity, bringing all the conveniences of running water, electricity, and paved roads. At the same time, centuries-old histories told in the old stone homes and terraced farms of these villages are simply erased.

In addition, this grand-scale development means providing ever-more energy to fuel the country. Urban residents in China use two and half times more energy than their rural counterparts. China is building one new coal-fired power plant every week to meet the demand; and land is being appropriated—often illegally and with little thought paid to agricultural needs or environmental protection—to construct new cities and new industries that also demand greater, resource-intensive inputs such as steel, timber, and cement. Throughout the country, the land is increasingly pockmarked and stripped as coal mines proliferate and the search for other minerals and ores to grow the economy continues.

The greatest cost of this vast geographic experiment, however, is only beginning to be known. China's land and resources are signaling their inability to withstand such an assault. The country's water resources are not replenishing themselves at a rate to sustain such growth. Lakes and rivers are evaporating. In Qinghai, which provides almost 50 percent of the water for the Yellow River and 25 percent of the water for the Yangtze River, more than two thousand lakes have simply dried up over the past few decades. Sixty million people in China have difficulty getting enough water for their daily needs. Cities and towns all along China's wealthy coast are sinking as cities drain underground aquifers of their water, causing severe subsidence. In Xian, home of the Terra Cotta Warriors, local officials reported at one point that they had lost $250 million in industrial output due to a lack of water. Officials throughout the country worry that they don't have enough water to run their factories and grow their economies.

China's land is also increasingly degraded and unable to support the country's growing demand for food. With 25 percent of the land technically desert and the desert advancing at a rate of 1,900 square miles per year, grasslands and fertile land are shrinking at an alarming rate. Even Beijing has become concerned about the encroaching Gobi desert, now only 125 miles away. China's traditionally rich biodiversity is also disappearing at a rate almost twice that of the world average.

The country's powerful rivers and their tributaries also have been transformed into a sprawling sewage system for the waste produced by the country's unfettered development. Small-scale township and village enterprises—the backbone of China's rapid economic growth in rural China—are dotted all along China's major rivers and their tributaries. Without environmental controls, these small factories simply drain their wastewater directly into the nearest rivers and streams. Foaming with pollution, these black and brown waterways now only rarely resemble the picture postcard beauty of Yuandang Lake in Xiamen or the Li River that flows through Guilin. Even more tragically, half of the Chinese people now drink polluted water; and 190 million of them drink water that is so contaminated it is making them ill. All along China's rivers and tributaries, villages and towns report startlingly high rates of cancer and tumors.

Even worse may be yet to come. The tens of thousands of glaciers on the Qinghai-Tibetan plateau are disappearing at an alarming rate of as much as 7 percent per year. Crop yields are anticipated to fall by 5–10 percent by 2030. Rising sea levels as a result of global climate change threaten to increase flooding in the Yellow, Yangtze, and Pearl River deltas, affecting the wealthiest and most densely populated regions of the country. The land appears to be transforming of its own accord.

The geography of China retains some of the most spectacular natural beauty and diversity in the world, despite the toll the land has incurred from centuries of war, population pressure, and economic development. Increasingly, however, the ability of the country's natural resources to replenish themselves is in doubt. China's leaders and people have recognized this challenge and have begun to discuss the need for a new approach. It will require both great vision and great will, however, to reverse a drive for development and relationship to the land that have defined Chinese history for centuries. Only over the course of the next century, as we continue to follow the evolution of China's geography, however, will we know whether a new course was truly and successfully charted. ■

MICHAEL S. YAMASHITA

The Great Wall—a monumental series of walls—was erected over the centuries to thwart invaders.
NEAR BEIJING, 1998

A bridge at the Summer Palace
BEIJING, 1997

GEORG GERSTER
**Terraced rice fields surround
a traditional village.**
GUIZHOU PROVINCE, 2006

Ascent of Gasherbrum II
CHINA-PAKISTAN BORDER, 1982

Rural Life: Green terraced hillsides, verdant farmland, and quaint villages are just some of the images that rural China conjures for many outside the country. Within China, however, there is a very different understanding. Quiet. Poor. Uneducated. Dirty. Politically weak. These are adjectives many urban Chinese might use to describe their rural counterparts. Even as China presents a united front to the rest of the world, the country is increasingly divided into two very separate societies: urban and rural, rich and poor. Tens of millions of migrant laborers move between the two worlds, but the families they leave behind face a very difficult life. China has the highest rate of female suicide in the world, with the ingestion of pesticide the most common path in rural China. Everything comes later to rural China—the development of infrastructure, provision of social services, and the advancement of the rule of law. Official corruption flourishes as does social unrest. At times, the number of rural protesters reaches into the tens of thousands, serving as a potent reminder to China's leaders and the wealthy elite of their historic roots and the traditional role of peasants as the revolutionary vanguard. E. E.

ROBERT GLENN KETCHUM
**Whitewashed walls and black tile roofs
are typical of houses in the Suzhou area.**
SUZHOU, SHANGHAI, 1987

41

DAVID BUTOW
Nanjing Road on a rainy night
SHANGHAI, 2006

City Life: Urbanizing hundreds of millions of people is a chaotic process. Construction dust is everywhere. Jackhammers begin at dawn and run till late in the evening. Red Xs are spray painted onto buildings about to be razed. Giant excavation sites give way to gleaming new office buildings and apartment complexes. Ring roads circle these new cities, one on top of the other, pushing further and further out into what was previously the Chinese countryside. Private cars clog the roads. Artistic and cultural communities emerge, pushing the boundaries of social change. Shops, galleries, and restaurants squeeze in to offer the necessary amenities and luxuries for the newly prosperous. Crime rises. Meanwhile, the migrants who have built the cities remain marginalized. With their different dialects, burnt skin, and shabby clothes, they live in poor shanty communities, with little opportunity to enjoy the fruits of their labor. **E. E.**

MICHAEL WOLF

**Dishes by the dozen remain after a
Cantonese family has finished their
Sunday meal.**
SOUTHERN CHINA, 2000

DANIELE MATTIOLI
**A view of the street through
a restaurant's fish tank**
SHANGHAI, 2003

MACDUFF EVERTON

**Looking from Kowloon across
Victoria Harbor to Hong Kong island**
HONG KONG, 1998

PAUL CHESLEY
**Bicycle traffic whizzes past
a giant billboard.**
SHANGHAI, 2000

IAN BERRY

Along the Yangtze River, a trader travels the old mountain road, in use for thousands of years.
SICHUAN PROVINCE, 2002

Three Gorges Dam: The dam is a massive cement structure, breathtaking in its size and in the audacity of its engineering. It is the largest hydroelectric power dam in the world, but only the most recent in a long line of grand-scale projects in China that not only tame the country's waterways but also serve as a testament to the egos of the leaders. The dam will provide more than 18,000 MW of power, transmitting electricity from the center of the country as far east as Shanghai. While the grandeur of the dam is undeniable, its construction has left much unresolved. Hundreds of thousands of Chinese farmers who were relocated from their now submerged villages remain jobless and without fair compensation for their loss of home and livelihood. At least two fish species that made their home only in the Yangtze are now extinct. Ancient cultural relics were lost forever when the reservoir was flooded. The failure to develop an adequate number of waste-treatment facilities has led to fears that the reservoir will soon become a cesspool. And the greatest, perhaps most unresolved, concern of all is that the dam will in fact be rendered useless in the next few decades by the heavy sedimentation of this mighty river. **E. E.**

JAMES WHITLOW DELANO

Top

A day laborer descends to the waterfront, which will be inundated by the third and final stage of flooding.
CHONGQING, SICHUAN PROVINCE, 2003

Bottom

A Wushan resident climbs up through the debris of the old town as demolition proceeds below.
WUSHAN, SICHUAN PROVINCE, 2003

JAMES WHITLOW DELANO

Top

Migrants are waiting to scavenge metal exposed by a shovel.
WUSHAN, SICHUAN PROVINCE, 2003

Bottom

A girl examines herself in a mirror while workers demolish her home.
WUSHAN, SICHUAN PROVINCE, 2003

ALESSANDRO DIGAETANO
A new 1,180-kilometer railway is the first to link the Tibet Autonomous Region with the rest of China.
QINGHAI PROVINCE, 2003

Border Regions: Beijing's border provinces present both a great opportunity and a great challenge. Many, such as Yunnan, Xinjiang, and Inner Mongolia, are rich in much-needed resources: timber, coal, natural gas, and minerals. At the same time, they raise serious political concerns. Home to many of the country's non-Han, ethnic minorities, with their own languages, cultures, religions, and dress, Beijing worries about the political loyalty of many within these provinces. It has tried to bind these provinces more closely to the rest of the country through investment and the relocation of Han Chinese to ensure greater control. But they risk a growing resentment as Tibetans and Uygurs sense—rightly or wrongly—that the Han Chinese are extracting their resources for the benefit of the rest of the country and seizing all the best economic opportunities. A similar challenge arises across the borders of these border regions. Myanmar, Kazakhstan, Russia, and Mongolia have all proved important resource-rich partners in China's effort to continue to fuel its rapidly growing economy. These borders are increasingly porous, trade flows freely, and people move back and forth with great ease. Yet local communities fear being overwhelmed by a large and permanent influx of Chinese. Even more challenging, alongside the rapidly growing licit economic relationship is a booming illicit trade in timber, drugs, sex, and even children. **E. E.**

SHARRON LOVELL

**A North Korean fishes on the banks
of the Yalu River.**
BORDER TOWN OF SINUIJU, 2006

**Kazak herders watch a dancer
perform at a circumcision ceremony
in the Altay Mountains.**
XINJIANG, UYGUR PROVINCE, 1996

Three old men have tea in the Uzum district of Turpan.
TURPAN, XINJIANG, UYGUR PROVINCE, 1995

BENOIT AQUIN

**A herder stands on parched earth
during a dust storm in Wuwei Oasis,
at the edge of the Tengger Desert.**
HEXI CORRIDOR, GANSU PROVINCE, 2006

Desertification: With the Gobi desert now at Beijing's doorstep, Chinese scientists and people are working feverishly to combat the seemingly relentless loss of fertile land and grasslands. At stake is the livelihood of millions of Chinese farmers, as well as the challenge of accommodating those millions who will march eastward to the coastal provinces in search of a new life and means of supporting themselves. When the traditional annual spring sandstorms hit northern China, airports close, roads become impassable and houses and even villages that are in the path of these ferocious sandstorms are practically submerged in sand. Moratoriums on cutting down trees for firewood, massive tree planting campaigns, and even bans on farming and herding in some areas are all under way. The desert, nonetheless, seems unwilling to change its course. There is a bright side, however. The Chinese people are turning adversity into opportunity: the newest rage in China's north—sand lake theme parks for tourists. E. E.

ALESSANDRO DIGAETANO

The Tianmo, a desert formed in recent years, is advancing toward Beijing. Visitors can slide down the dunes on sleds.
HEBEI PROVINCE, 2006

ALESSANDRO DIGAETANO
**Weather specialists used chemicals
to engineer Beijing's rainfall and
lightning to relieve drought and
rinse away dust.**
BEIJING, 2006

BENOIT AQUIN

With a statue of Genghis Khan as a backdrop, pedestrians in the city of Xilinhot obey a stoplight during a dust storm.
XILINGOL STEPPE,
INNER MONGOLIA, 2006

china: History

History: In the spring of 1895, many of China's best and brightest were gathered in Beijing to take the triennial exam that would allow them to attain the highest degree available, to be "presented scholars" (*jinshi*). It was at this time that the final, humiliating terms of the Treaty of Shimonoseki, the treaty that concluded the Sino-Japanese War of 1894–1895, were announced: an indemnity of over 200 million taels (ounces) of silver, the opening up of new treaty ports, and the ceding "in perpetuity" of Taiwan. The young, learned, and increasingly nationalistic degree candidates were outraged by the imperial court's willingness to sign such a treaty. Led by the brilliant but emotional Kang Youwei, the scholars drew up a long petition to the emperor pleading to continue the war and enact radical change at home.

There was something fundamentally modern about this petition movement. It brought together the themes of nationalism, student activism, and radicalism that would dominate Chinese politics for most of the next century. In 1898 Kang Youwei and his fellow radical reformers would have their chance to test out their approaches when the young Guangxu emperor, then 24, began to assert his majority against the dominating presence of his aunt, the Empress Dowager Cixi, by inviting Kang and others to the court. The idealistic emperor hoped Kang could effect rapid modernization of China, but when Kang and his fellow reformers launched a broadside at everything from the educational system to the organization of the bureaucracy to even the continuing influence of the Empress Dowager, the opposition became too much. After a mere hundred days, Kang was forced to flee Beijing as the reform movement came crashing to a halt.

Even as Kang was challenging the patterns of the past from above, Sun Yat-sen, a more marginal figure in traditional terms, was forming revolutionary organizations, determined to throw out the Manchu overlords and implement democracy in China. Sun's efforts bore fruit in 1911 when a bomb exploded prematurely in a foreign concession area in the city of Wuhan, leading to the abdication of the boy emperor Puyi, the establishment of a republic, and the naming of Yuan Shikai, a military official with no connection to the revolutionary movement, as the first president of the Republic of China.

Yuan Shikai had no democratic sentiment whatsoever. He sought to consolidate central government control, then slipping badly particularly in the south where the revolution had its greatest strength, and more fatally tried to establish a new dynasty with himself as emperor. Provinces began to declare independence, and, as civil war brewed, Yuan Shikai died in June 1916. His death, however, did not spare the nation civil war. With dynastic legitimacy gone and the young republic in tatters, military leaders began to compete with each other for territory and riches, the biggest prize being Beijing.

The themes of domestic disorder, imperialism, radical idealism, and populist passions, evident in the very different movements of Kang Youwei and Sun Yat-sen at the turn of the century, were manifested in different form when the allied powers met in Paris following the conclusion of World War I. Despite Woodrow Wilson's calls for "self determination" and "making the world safe for democracy" that had inspired a generation of young Chinese, the decision-makers yielded to Japan's demands that Germany's territorial concessions in Shandong Province be turned over to

Japan. Beleaguered warlords, desirous of Japanese loans, had "gladly agreed" in a secret protocol to transfer these rights to Japan. When word of this decision was transmitted back to China, students at Beijing University took to the streets to protest. The "May Fourth Movement," as this patriotic and idealistic movement became known, paved the way for a new and broader wave of nationalism and anti-imperialism. The decision taken at Versailles unintentionally created a situation in which Lenin's message would be heard by increasing numbers of Chinese.

The Bolshevik revolution had occurred only a year and a half earlier. Inspired by this revolutionary success, Li Dazhao, the librarian at Beijing University, began to form Marxist study groups and study Marxism. In May 1919, just as students were most impassioned, Li published a highly influential essay declaring himself a Marxist and laying out his views. The Chinese Communist Party, with help from the Soviet Union, was founded two years later. Mao Zedong, already an experienced activist in his native Hunan province, was one of the 13 delegates who attended that inaugural congress in Shanghai.

The May Fourth Movement not only led to the founding of the Chinese Communist Party, it also reenergized Sun Yat-sen's Nationalist Party. In 1924, again with Soviet assistance, the Nationalist Party was reorganized and the nascent Communist Party admitted. The Comintern (Communist International) argued that China was not ready for a socialist revolution, and until the time was right, the Communist Party could help the Nationalists in their quest for a "bourgeois democratic" revolution. Chiang Kai-shek, soon to head the Nationalist Party, was named commandant of the newly established Whampoa Military Academy where offi-

cers of a new Nationalist army would be trained. Zhou Enlai, later premier of China, was appointed political commissar.

The merger of the reinvigorated Nationalist Party and the small but energetic Communist Party was not one that could last. Sun Yat-sen was the glue that held this awkward alliance together, and when he died in 1925, tensions between the two parties began to simmer.

This tension broke open when Chiang Kai-shek and his Nationalist troops reached Shanghai in the spring of 1927. With the help of the city's notorious secret societies, he launched a "party purification movement" by slaughtering Communists and those merely alleged to be. By the time the movement was over, some 10,000 people were dead. The "first united front" between the Communists and the Nationalists had been brought to a bloody end.

Chiang Kai-shek won this round. The Nationalist capital was established in Nanjing (Nanking) in 1928, but the new government only had effective control over half a dozen provinces, mostly in the lower Yangzi valley, where Nanjing and Shanghai are located. Although he gradually extended Nationalist control, Chiang could not eliminate the Chinese Communist Party. After the crushing purge of party purification and other military defeats, Mao Zedong and a few other Communist leaders retreated to the mountainous terrain of the Jinggang Mountains in southern Jiangxi Province.

In Jiangxi, Mao and his fellow Communists developed guerrilla tactics, mobilized people in peasant associations, built an army around Communist cadres, and learned to integrate Marxism with the realities of rural life. As the movement expanded, and as Communist leaders still living in Shanghai came under ever greater pressures, the party's top leaders moved to Jiangxi, pushing Mao aside. This loss of power may have saved Mao's political life. In a series of "extermination campaigns," Chiang Kai-shek applied ever greater military pressure on the Communist base area in Jiangxi, finally forcing the Communists to break out of the encirclement and head for the mountainous areas of the southwest.

This military debacle was the start of the "Long March." En route, in January 1935, the leadership was able to pause in a poor county seat in the mountainous province of Guiyang to sort out leadership issues. In a long speech, Mao blamed the loss of the base area in Jiangxi on the military tactics of the leadership who had forced him from power. When the meeting was over, Mao was appointed to a three-person military body that would oversee strategy and tactics. Mao was on his way back.

The Long March finally ended nearly a year after its start in the poor northwestern town of Yanan. This became the Communist's revolutionary capital and it was where Mao began to systematically develop and impose his own particular brand of Marxism—Mao Zedong Thought—on the growing Communist movement.

Confronted with the threat—and soon the reality—of Japanese invasion, those two great antagonists, Mao Zedong and Chiang Kai-shek, joined forces once again in an uneasy "second united front." By 1941 the united front was over in everything but name, and when the war finally ended U.S. Secretary of State George C. Marshall headed to China to see if he could prevent civil war. He could not, and a war-ravaged country again plunged into bloody conflict.

When it was over, Mao Zedong, on October 1, 1949, stood upon the rostrum at Tiananmen Square and proclaimed the found-ing of the People's Republic of China. There were great hopes for peace, stability, and the social and economic reconstruction of a nation torn by a century of imperialism, civil war, deprivation, and revolution. The Chinese people, however, were not to be blessed with peace and prosperity. Family farming gave way to collectiviza-tion and then communization as Mao Zedong, intent on "overtak-ing Britain and catching up to the United States," plunged the country into the great mobilization of the "Great Leap Forward." Peasants were mobilized to build "backyard furnaces"; efforts to fuel such furnaces despoiled the environment and exhausted the population. Faked pictures of children sitting on wheat that was said to grow dense enough and strong enough to hold them up could not hide forever the tragic failures of the leap, as some 30 million people perished from famine and related diseases.

Disaster was not enough to convince Mao Zedong to change his mind. Only five years after the end of the leap, in 1966, Mao unleashed one more paroxysm of chaos on the land. Red Guards were called on to carry out a "Cultural Revolution" against the "four olds" (old customs, old habits, old culture, and old thinking). Students rose up against their teachers, factory workers against their bosses, and the "masses" against their rulers. Intellectuals and "capitalist roaders" were marched through the streets in dunce caps, beaten, sometimes killed, and sent to jails or the countryside to "learn from the peasants." The madness did not end until Mao breathed his last on September 9, 1976. Only a month later, his wife, the former actress turned radical leader Jiang Qing, and three colleagues were arrested as the "Gang of Four." These four would serve as symbols for the violence and chaos of the Cultural

Revolution, preserving Mao as the great leader who had led the revolution against imperialism and feudalism.

Deng Xiaoping, twice purged by Mao, emerged as China's new strongman. A practical man deeply frustrated by the ideological cant of the Cultural Revolution, he was determined to get China's economy moving. Deng's timing was good. He welcomed foreign investment just as Hong Kong manufacturers were finding labor costs too high; many company heads moved their manufacturing activities into neighboring Guangdong Province where they had family ties. "Special Economic Zones" were set up in Shenzhen and three other localities to welcome foreign investment. Eventually other places, including the eastern part of Shanghai (Pudong) were opened up to foreign and Chinese investment, transforming the skylines of cities that had hardly changed since the 1930s. Private enterprises were allowed to grow, and state-owned enterprises, the core of the old socialist economy, produced a smaller and smaller percentage of China's industrial output.

Economic reform took off and it clearly bettered the lives of people, lifting millions out of poverty, enriching a few, and creating a nascent middle class. But economic reform also created uncertainty. Inflation was a new and scary phenomenon. And jobs were threatened as state-owned enterprises began hiring laborers on contracts rather than as lifetime employees. Intellectuals were increasingly frustrated by defenders of the old system, and a new generation of students took the gains of the past decade for granted and pushed for new freedoms. It was a combustible mixture, especially as Deng aged and there was obvious jockeying for succession. When the liberal former party head, Hu Yaobang, died suddenly on April 15, 1989, it was like a match thrown on dried tinder. Once again students took to the streets in protest. After six weeks of indecision and infighting at the highest levels of the system, the army finally put a brutal stop to the movement.

The trauma of the crackdown in and around Tiananmen Square shocked political leaders, students, and those who watched from around the world. China began to recover slowly, but too slowly for Deng Xiaoping, once dubbed the little man in a hurry. In 1992 Deng was 88 years old, and he was determined to inject vigor in his reform movement one last time. So that January, he headed to China's symbol of reform and opening, the Shenzhen Special Economic Zone, where he denounced conservative politicians in unsparing terms. The economy, spurred by a binge of investment, took off again, especially in old cities such as Shanghai, while new cities grew up with dizzying speed. Modernization was hitting China with full force, but as the bright city lights dazzled the eyes and as fortunes were made, the gap with the agricultural hinterland was growing dangerously. Not unlike in Mao Zedong's youth, peasants were beginning to organize and protest. Workers laid off from state-owned enterprises likewise took to the streets. A new sense of rights consciousness was sweeping across the land.

A century after Kang Youwei organized his fellow exam takers, China had emerged as a power with global interests and as an increasingly wealthy nation, though more so in absolute than in per capita terms. The old dream of wealth and power was being realized, but questions of political participation, citizenship, equality, national identity, and China's role in the world are still being debated and fought over. ■

74

HENRI CARTIER-BRESSON
The Forbidden City in the morning mist, a few days before the Communists' arrival
BEIJING, December 1948

Imperial Past: With the world's oldest continuous civilization, it is perhaps no wonder that the only way China was going to shake off the weight of that imperial tradition was through revolutionary change. A century of revolution and, finally, economic development has so changed the face of China that this imperial past hardly seems relevant. But as you travel through a province like Henan, where ancient tombs dot the landscape, or as you climb on the Great Wall or walk slowly through the Forbidden City, you feel the reality of that past. As the Communist revolution fades, there is a reawakening of a consciousness of China's past. Television series recounting China's emperors have become popular. There is a renewed pride in China's past, a pride that mingles perhaps too easily with nationalism. The Empress Dowager and bound feet are gone forever, but ancient civilizations do not disappear without a trace. One of the most difficult tasks in contemporary China is to reconcile a revolution that took "strike down Confucius' shop" as one of its hallmarks with Confucius himself. Confucius' family home and tomb have been restored, and the establishment of "Confucius Institutes" abroad to teach Chinese language and culture suggest a continuing vitality to China's traditions. **J. F.**

HIROJI KUBOTA
Opposite
**Grave site of the emperors of the
Northern Song dynasty**
SONGXIAN, HENAN PROVINCE, 1982

PHOTOGRAPHER UNKNOWN
**Cixi, the Empress Dowager of China,
(1835–1908)**
BEIJING, 19th century

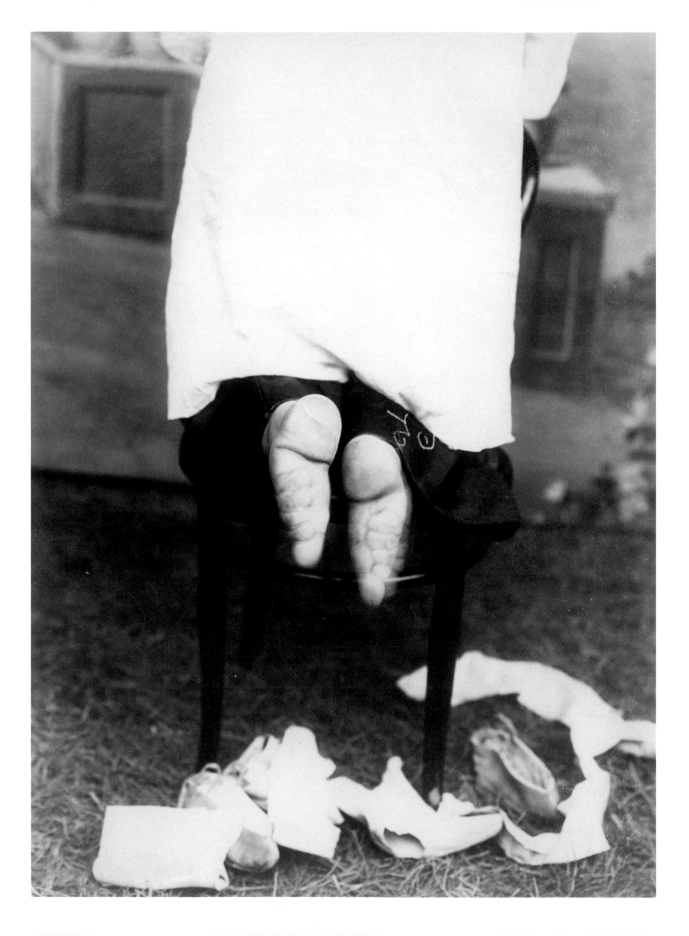

PHOTOGRAPHER UNKNOWN
Opposite
**The Wang Lung Gate steps lead from
the ferry to the business district.**
CHONGQING, SICHUAN PROVINCE, 1944

ALFRED T. PALMER
Street scene
HONG KONG, 1930s

87

Nationalists: Nationalism has been the leitmotif of modern Chinese politics. Sun Yat-sen's Three Principles of the People—democracy, nationalism, and the people's livelihood—articulated a vision of an elite led, quasi-democratic polity defending the rights of the nation against the indignities of imperialism and pursuing social justice for the people. After Sun died, Chiang Kai-shek grasped Sun's idea of the need for a period of "tutelage"—a period in which the people could be educated in the Three Principles of the People and how to exercise their democratic rights—but never got around to implementing democracy. Chiang's failure was rooted in his military background, which led him to lean heavily on China's army to reinforce his leadership, as well as in the difficult realities of the day residual warlordism, the Communist movement, and the all-too-real threat from Japan. The Japanese invasion in 1937 postponed any notion of implementing democracy at least until the end of World War II, and then the specter of civil war was upon China. Nationalism has been a constant, but it has often been used to stifle democratic urges. **J. F.**

Gen. Chiang Kai-shek,
president of China
NANJING, JIANGSU PROVINCE, 1933

ROBERT CAPA

Female Nationalist Army cadets train in Hankou, where Gen. Chiang Kai-shek retreated from Japanese troops.
HANKOU, 1938

As Beijing is surrounded by Communist troops, the Kuomintang calls some 10,000 troops to arms.
BEIJING, December 1948

Street of antique dealers

HENRI CARTIER-BRESSON
**Pigtailed students stride to class
in the engineering school.**
SHENYANG, LIAONING PROVINCE, 1958

During one of many famines, Chinese children queue to receive rations.
PLACE UNKNOWN, 1930

Communists: It is easy to forget the sense of optimism that Chinese felt in 1949 as Mao Zedong declared that "the Chinese people have stood up" and declared the establishment of the People's Republic of China. The leftist writer Hu Feng wrote a long poem called "Time has now Begun" celebrating the optimism of the era. Recalling these events many years later, Li Shenzhi, the dean of American studies in China, called these words "inspired" and exactly the right words to express the moment. Hu Feng was a protégé of China's most celebrated writer, Lu Xun, but neither pedigree nor leanings saved him. Only six years after he extolled the Communist victory, Mao Zedong would accuse Hu Feng of heading a "counter-revolutionary clique." Hu languished in jail for the next quarter century, dying three years before his name could be cleared. Li Shenzhi was a bright young man of 26 when he witnessed the founding of the People's Republic, but he nevertheless found himself following in the footsteps of the more famous Hu. In 1957 Li was named a rightist. Like many others, he did not return to public life until after Mao died. The Chinese revolution, like other revolutionary movements, devoured its own children. **J. F.**

LI ZHENSHENG

Thousands from Harbin's University of Industry celebrate Mao's first meeting with citizens to celebrate the Cultural Revolution.
HARBIN, HEILONGJIANG PROVINCE,
August 12, 1966

WU YINXIAN

Mao Zedong delivers a speech honoring the "labor heroes" of the Shaanxi-Gansu-Ningxia border region.
PLACE UNKNOWN, 1943

LI ZHENSHENG

Opposite

During the Cultural Revolution, an official is forced to wear a dunce cap and a placard with the accusatory label "black gang element."
HARBIN, HEILONGJIANG PROVINCE, 1966

JACQUET-FRANCILLON

Employees of a hotel operate a steel smelting furnace in the courtyard in support of the Great Leap Forward.
BEIJING, 1958

Bamboo Curtain: Isolation was not good for China. And the isolation got worse before it got better. With the campaign to "Resist America and Aid Korea" China's isolation from the Western world increased and its political and ideological control of the people reached deeper. Hundreds of thousands were killed or jailed, and those who were not were cowed into silence. "Mao Zedong Thought" became the only guideline. In the cities, private shops were closed; "work units" (danwei) took over socioeconomic life, dispensing housing and other benefits as they saw fit. Peasants were deprived of most of their land as the rest was collectivized, then communized. Political movements periodically pulsated across the land, making examples of this person or that class. Half a million intellectuals were sent to the countryside in the Anti-Rightist Movement of 1957. Families were often set against each other, trying to survive by denouncing each other, hoping to protect the children. Yet families and individuals inevitably resisted and survived. When political movements relaxed, individuals and families rebounded. When the political movements had finally exhausted themselves and Mao had died, families were restored and individuals were ready to make their way in a new world. Scares remained and values were diminished, but individuals and families strove to find security and meaning in a new world. **J. F.**

**Students marching in
Tiananmen Square**
BEIJING, 1965

JOHN DOMINIS

**U.S. President Richard Nixon and
Chinese Premier Zhou Enlai share
a toast at a banquet.**
BEIJING, 1972

ELLIOT ERWITT

Top

Premier Deng Xiaoping enjoys a rodeo during a visit to Houston, Texas.
TEXAS, U.S.A., 1979

PHOTOGRAPHER UNKNOWN

Bottom

Early in his career, Deng Xiaoping (second from left), who became China's paramount leader not long after Mao Zedong's death, was a political commissar in the Communist army.
SHANXI PROVINCE, 1938

GUY LE QUERREC

**Yung An Road seen from the
Hotel Chien Men**
BEIJING, 1984

Protests: The children of the revolution. China's modern history has been punctuated and defined by its protests. Kang Youwei led degree candidates to memorialize the emperor in protest against the terms of the Treaty of Shimonoseki. The boycott against American goods in 1905 protesting the Chinese Exclusion Act was perhaps the first expression of popular nationalism. The May Fourth Movement in 1919 gave definition to intellectual protest and laid out a set of ideals—democracy and science—that have stood in silent judgment of later political movements. The May 30th Movement of 1925, protesting the killing of a Chinese worker in a Japanese plant, marked a shift from intellectual leadership to popular leadership. Nationalistic protests in the 1930s and 1940s radicalized a generation of students and helped usher the Chinese nationalists out of mainland Chinese history. But the Communist victory did not stop protest. Students and workers took to the street in 1957, and the Red Guards that took to the streets in the Cultural Revolution embodied a pent-up anger. More demonstrations came in 1985, 1986, and, of course, in 1989. Although smaller in scale and less dramatic than these protests, demonstrations of one sort or another are a characteristic of contemporary Chinese life. J. F.

china: Tradition

Tradition: Tradition is something that is at once readily observed and intangible. The Chinese boast of several thousand years of continuous cultural tradition, but what can be observed today in China as indications of tradition are usually relics of the past. In daily life, tradition survives mainly in the intangibles.

There is, for example, no traditional form of dress that one can see on the streets. As in most other countries in Asia, most people dress in the mass-produced clothes manufactured on the orders of multinational companies, and often crafted by the people wearing them. This is understandable in terms of modernization, Westernization, or as a matter of economy. What is exceptional in China is that there is no longer a "national dress," as there is in other Asian countries. This causes a major dilemma on ceremonial occasions such as weddings and for statesmen and diplomats attending formal events on the international stage.

The cause of this is easy to trace. When the Manchus came in from the Northeast in the mid-17th century and took over the rule of the empire, all men were required to abandon their national dress and wear Manchu-style clothes together with the "pigtail." (Women were spared this indignity.) After the 1911 revolution, when the Qing dynasty of the Manchus was overthrown, there was the Zhongshan dress, so-named after Sun Zhongshan (Sun Yat-sen), the founder of modern China. This jacket was adopted by Mao and the Communists and was then known to the rest of the world as the "Mao jacket." When people were liberated from the rigidity of early Communist rule, the Mao jacket was rapidly and spontaneously discarded in favor of Western (or international) style of dress—a suit and tie for formal occasions.

The nonagenarian scholar Ji Shanlin, a renowned specialist in ancient Indian and Central Asian languages, complains repeatedly in recent years in his occasional writing that the young people are too easily swayed by fashion (implying that there is a loss of tradition or national identity) and that he himself would henceforth wear only the Zhongshan jacket. For women, the problem is not as acute, as they have recourse to the more or less straight gown with slits on the sides, which nevertheless is derived from the Manchu gown—as evidenced by its former name: qipao, meaning "banner robe," the banner referring to the Manchu. Men used also to wear the long straight gown, with a short jacket on top for formal events, and a cap to cover the shaved front part of the skull. But this form of attire has not been seen for some time now. What has survived is the pajamas-style loose jacket and trousers that used to be worn under the long gown. Practitioners of martial arts, including taiji exercises that one sees being practiced by large numbers of people in the early morning in open spaces, still wear them. The outer gown is sometimes worn for effect. There is talk of a costumes research institute in Shanghai that is engaged in the design of a national dress, but as yet there has been no announcement of a result.

Where one does see "traditional dress" is on Buddhist monks. But the impression one gets nowadays is that the Buddhist robes are made and worn like theater costumes. This impression is strongest when one encounters monks in secular settings, and is indelible even when a ceremony or procession is in progress.

GILLES SABRIÉ
Preceding Pages
**An opera troupe comes to a small
village in the mountains.**
SHANXI PROVINCE, 2005

Perhaps such impression is partly generated in the mind of the observer and partly the reflection of an aspect of reality.

What does look more authentic is the behavior of worshippers in Buddhist temples. The way people kneel in front of the statues of deities, the pious look on their faces, and the gestures of worship seem timeless. Less authentic are the statues of deities, for nearly all of them in urban areas were destroyed during the Cultural Revolution and remodeled, not according to canon or any knowledge of Buddhist iconography, but by craftsmen or students of art academies who freely sculpted after photographs of what was there before. And then, what is enshrined in Buddhist temples are not necessarily all images of Buddhas, Bodhisattvas, or Lohans, but also Daoist (Taoist) immortals or gods of popular religion—like Guandi, the god of war. It makes no difference to the faithful; all deities in temples are worshiped irrespective of their origin or affiliation. This is a true tradition in Chinese religious practice, going back for centuries. It matters not whom you worship, as long as your prayer is answered. The indiscrimination goes further. Not only does one find images of Daoist immortals in Buddhist temples, but people worship as comfortably in Lamaist (Tibetan Buddhist) temples as in one of any other Buddhist sect. It is also possible not to find the image of the Buddha associated with a particular sect in a temple supposedly of the sect—no Amitabha, for example, in a "Pure Land" temple in Hong Kong.

Buddhist monks live well nowadays, as evidenced by their presence in the dining rooms of luxury hotels. This is not new. Monks of the Tang dynasty in rich temples were granted vast tracts of land, and a large number of servants also lived well, but also in a highly cultivated style. Tea drinking, said to have begun as a way of keeping meditating monks awake, became a refined activity. The eighth century lay Buddhist Lu Yü, who spent much of his time in monasteries, became known for the *Tea Classic*, in which he discussed varieties of tea, water (rating all the known springs), tea making and drinking, and the utensils, including the relative merit of ceramic tea bowls from various kilns. The last part has been a useful reference for students of the history of Chinese ceramics. There has been a recent revival of the cult of tea (not that it ever was interrupted for long) in private homes and establishments catering to tourists. However, in the present revival, there is a suspicion of pretense, if not pretension, rather than refined delectation. For one thing, water from unpolluted springs is one of the rarest commodities in present-day China. However, the growing interest in tea does have the effect of encouraging greater care in the production of tea for the market, resulting in better quality on the whole, with a corresponding surge in price.

Food has always been a major concern in China and is what every visitor to the country must confront. It is important in two ways: as cultural expression and as a basic consideration in the formulation of state policy. The former is a matter of consumption, and the latter that of production. For the time being, we live in one of the rare periods in Chinese history when food production or provision is not a serious problem. All attention is focused on consumption in the rich cities, especially those in coastal areas. One enters in amazement into mammoth restaurants on the ground floor, where one finds a vast emporium of everything edible, animal or vegetable, wild or domesticated. On the upper floors are open restaurants, banquet halls, and private dining rooms of various sizes, accommodating parties of hundreds to a few. These restaurants, one is told, originated in the city of Ningpo in Zhejiang province, long known as an entreport of maritime trade, and are now to be found in major cities such as Nanjing. Many legendary tales are told of the exquisite and extravagant cuisine in Hangzhou in the 12th century when it was the capital of the Southern Song dynasty. It seems that cities like Shanghai, and Hangzhou itself, will enter history books on the same account.

There are aspects of banqueting in present day China which are steeped in a tradition that nobody likes but everybody endures. These have mainly to do with the welcoming banquet and the farewell banquet for a visitor who may be a senior official or a foreign guest of high standing. The custom is probably as old as China itself, but the lavishness and nomenclature would vary at different times and in different regions. During the Yuan dynasty (1279–1368), when the Mongols ruled China, they were known as the "dismounting banquet" and "mounting the horse banquet," and today these terms are still used in Inner Mongolia, only that the visiting officials mount and dismount from airplanes and limousines and often visit a city a day. This vastly decreases the intervals between banquets, which often causes complaints from both hosts and guests. Still, the practice is carried on inexorably. And the feasting is not confined to the above mentioned occasions. There are many other events that require celebration by feasting. The great poet of the 11th century, Su Shi, when he was governor of Hangzhou, described the city as "hell of food and wine." And this was before Hangzhou became the capital. Many foreign visitors to China would experience a taste of this culture, especially if they are on a strict schedule of traveling to a number of cities.

The wedding feast used to be the grandest of all, followed by celebrations of important birthdays. In the old days, wedding expenses, including the banquet, would often lead to heavy debt. However, with rapid changes in social conditions and mores, and the relative ease of marriage and divorce, not all weddings are nowadays celebrated with the same extravagance. Similarly, the elaborate rituals associated with weddings, as remembered by the elder generation about to pass away or as recorded by social anthropologists, is now enacted episodically only in movies. Traditional wedding attire, especially for the bride, which survived longer than daily wear, is also on the point of extinction.

One feature of Chinese commerce, which has not only survived but manifested in ever larger scale, is the concentration of a particular trade in one street or district—a permanent urban fair. There are book cities in large buildings where all publishers have their own stands, like in a department store. In Beijing there is a Curio City. But the most spectacular are the garment districts, occupying a whole block or several blocks, with offices and shops in buildings and stalls in the streets blocking traffic. Here all wholesale and retail trade goes on, from large-scale transactions to the purchase of a T-shirt.

Street stalls, selling everything from cooked food to fruits and vegetables to knick-knacks, are reappearing everywhere in China after a period of strict control of all commerce in the hands of the government, testifying to the entrepreneurial spirit of the people and the demise of state-run enterprises that used to employ everybody.

Another traditional practice, perhaps not unique but certainly common in China, is the imitation or copying of well-known products. The copies were sold under names that were phonetically or graphologically close to the original brand name. Another way was to put on imitation products trademarks that could easily be mistaken for the original. One of the most famous examples of this practice was the proliferation of Wangmazi scissors in Beijing. The original brand of Wangmazi scissors was known in Beijing before the Qing dynasty (est. 1744). Until the early 20th century, numerous shops in Beijing were selling Wangmazi scissors, and others with similar sounding names or characters. Similarly, the faking of paintings and calligraphy by famous masters also has a long tradition in China, leading to the despair of collectors who have not developed the discerning eye that is sensitive to the different schools of fakes—with characteristics as distinctive as the originals. The relaxed attitude to what is nowadays known as "copyright infringement" is not shared by international corporations.

In a country that was formerly an empire, there had to be many cultural traditions that co-existed among different ethnic groups or communities in different provinces. There are, and have always been, mutual borrowings or adaptations. Take the simple example of food. There is no longer any pure regional food anywhere, at least not in restaurants. On the other hand, one can find "Cantonese" food in the Autonomous Region of Xinjiang (Chinese Central Asian) with ingredients flown in from Hong Kong. And in subtropical Hong Kong, one can sample "Mongolian hot-pot" along with cuisine from many parts of the world. Nothing is quite original, but everything is there everywhere. The rampant mutual access is bound to undermine local traditions. However, the most profound changes have come as a result of political, social, and economic forces which have already affected the appearance of things, from dress to architecture to the conduct of daily life. What for the moment persist are the intangibles, what is not obvious to the casual observer.

The costumes of actors on the Peking Opera stage may look nothing like anything that anybody wore in any period of Chinese history. Yet, under the scrutiny of an art or costumes historian, every detail of the costumes, from the ridiculously long feathers sported by the "barbarian" warriors to the stiff and large "belt" hanging loosely from the waist of the scholar official, can be traced somehow to sartorial fashion in some period of Chinese history going back centuries if not millennia.

But all this will disappear also, as the theater arts transform themselves following the introduction of Western opera, and opera houses are built in Shanghai and Beijing in what can only be viewed by the Chinese as outlandish styles of architecture. In no other period of Chinese history have there been so many radical changes in every aspect of life: political, social, and personal. Whatever the transformation ahead, some intangibles will remain. As to what they are, we shall have to wait and find out. ■

PAUL LOWE
In the early morning, the Tea House is filled with old men and fashionable youths.
SHANGHAI, 1997

A grandmother's hat indicates that she is a Hakka, a minority group in China.
SHENZHEN, GUANGDONG
PROVINCE, 1982

PHOTOGRAPHER UNKNOWN
**Women of Miao ethnic minority,
in traditional dress, wait to perform
a dance.**
LANGDESHANG VILLAGE,
GUIZHOU PROVINCE, 2006

MICHAEL WOLF

On Ancestor Day, women from the Bai tribe have just been to the temple to worship.
DALI, YUNNAN PROVINCE, 2003

Aging: The aging in China (say, 70 years and older), like others all over the world, are becoming a burden to society. They themselves also carry a burden. The former is social and economic, and the latter is historical. People who were born in 1937, the year of the Marco Polo Bridge incident, which marked the formal beginning of eight years of Sino-Japanese war and decades of hardship, would have parents who themselves were born in chaotic times of social and political transition, and their grandparents would certainly have been subjects of the Qing dynasty, which ended in 1911. They would have grown up with all the old customs and manners current in the old days, some as old as Chinese history. The keeping of crickets (for their "songs" and for fighting), for example, is an ancient pastime. The chief minister at the end of the Southern Song dynasty in the 13th century, Jia Sidao, wrote the earliest known treatise on crickets. The Xuande emperor (r. 1425–1435) of the Ming dynasty was another fanatic, and so was practically everybody else. The making of accessories for keeping crickets became an artistic industry. Old cricket cages in the form of decorated pottery jars, and molded gourds, are now collected as works of art. Nevertheless, nowadays interest in crickets is a sign of age. (Among other factors, many of the fields where children went to catch crickets are now sites for industrial complexes.) Mahjong, a game with antecedents going back only a few centuries, once universally popular, is also becoming less so, as the young have other distractions like video games. These activities will vanish with the present generation of old people, taking with them vestiges of ancient culture and memories of a tumultuous period of Chinese history. **J. C. Y. W.**

MICHAEL WOLF

Two crickets in the fight arena: Their handlers tease them into a fighting rage by tickling them with sticks.
SHANGHAI, 2002

DAVID BUTOW
**Tiger Hill, with Yu Yuan Pagoda
in the background**
SHANGHAI, 2006

GILLES SABRIÉ
**An opera troupe performs before
a captivated audience.**
SHANXI PROVINCE, 2005

Opera: There is no theater in China that is not for "opera"—drama acted out with mime, intoned recitations (in a standard old pronunciation not immediately understandable to the audience), some natural speech in local dialect, set-piece arias, and, in some plays, a great deal of fighting and acrobatics. (Quick qualification: in the early 20th century, with the first wave of Western influence, some excellent stage plays were written and performed in major cities, but the war intervened.) Storytelling, sometimes accompanied by music and singing, is an ancient art form of entertainment and edification in China, as in all cultures, but stage plays began relatively recently by Chinese standards. The earliest plays were probably Buddhist dramas introduced through Central Asia, and the general form of Chinese opera, in all its regional variations, came into shape sometime in the 12th century (or slightly earlier) and reached great popularity in the 13th to 14th centuries. Many famous plays were written by many writers during the Yuan dynasty (1279–1368) under Mongol rule in China, and most traditional operas performed today are based on or derived from plays of this period. Yuan drama was one of the earliest Chinese cultural exports. Voltaire, in the mid-18th century, based his play *The Orphan of China* on a famous Yuan drama, *The Orphan of Zhao*.

For centuries, when theater was the most popular form of entertainment, Chinese traveling troupes would perform all over the country, going from town to town, village to village. The props were reduced to the minimum—hence the importance of mime. The absence of props also focuses all attention on the actors: their acting, singing, costumes, and make-up. The audience members are knowledgeable and behave naturally, talking and eating most of the time, but, in moments of high drama, or when a great star begins an aria, the sudden silence is electric—to be broken by thundering calls of appreciation. This is the "total theater" transmitted to Europe by Bertolt Brecht, who adopted a Yuan drama for his *Caucasian Chalk Circle*, and also the empty Chinese stage. **J. C. Y. W.**

GILLES SABRIÉ
**Chinese opera usually includes
acrobatic scenes recreating battles.**
SHANXI PROVINCE, 2005

MICHAEL WOLF
**Schoolchildren sweep the school yard
each morning before lessons begin.**
YAN'AN, SHAANXI PROVINCE, 2003

Education: Education in traditional China consisted in large part of studying the classics, particularly the Four Books as interpreted by Neo-Confucianists of the 11th and 12th centuries. The scholarly elite would be familiar with all the 13 books in the classical canon and the dynastic histories. Philology and epigraphy would be part of the advanced study in the classics, and history would provide insights into the rise and fall of dynasties and lessons to be learned in statecraft. Education reform began in the late 19th century in the waning days of the Qing dynasty when textbooks were written for a curriculum similar to those of Western schools. Before the introduction of modern textbooks, the acquisition of learning beyond the Confucian canon was an uphill task. To be able to use a dictionary required considerable training in philology. General education was greatly hampered by wars in the first half of the 20th century, but the greatest damage to higher education was done by the Cultural Revolution, from which the universities are still struggling to recover. Nevertheless, at the most basic level, China has made great strides in recent decades. Literacy has spread to many rural areas and it is increasingly easier to be an auto-didact owing to the proliferation of introductory and reference books. However, the opportunity for a large section of the population to study has caused problems not unknown in other countries such as Japan. The immense pressure on students to attend elite schools and universities is increasingly creating psychological difficulties for children and parents. J. C. Y. W.

ALESSANDRO DIGAETANO

**A portrait of Karl Marx hangs on the
wall of a rural classroom.**
HUANGBAIYU, BENXI, LIAONING
PROVINCE, 2006

ALESSANDRO DIGAETANO

Top

Another example of China's rural-urban divide: Rural schools are often old and neglected.
BENXI, LIAONING PROVINCE, 2006

Bottom

Increasingly, students are taught English, as well as Chinese.
BENXI, LIAONING PROVINCE, 2006

Guided by her parents, a student of acrobatics practices contorting her body.
WU QIAO, HUBEI PROVINCE, 2003

Children carry on the local tradition in Hebei, birthplace of the Chinese art of acrobatics.
HEBEI PROVINCE, 2003

JUSTIN GUARIGLIA
Students practice synchronized kung fu at the Ta Gou academy.
HENAN PROVINCE, 2004

Tibetan women receive medicinal benefits by bathing in a hot-spring grotto outside Tongren.
QINGHAI PROVINCE, 2003

A member of a local cold-water swimming group prepares to jump from a diving board sculpted in ice.
HARBIN, HEILONGJIANG PROVINCE, 1999

ALEXA BRUNET

Top

Brightly colored lights illuminate ice-sculpted buildings at Harbin's annual ice festival.
HARBIN, HEILONGJIANG PROVINCE, 2005

Bottom

Harbin's city of ice attracts visitors from afar.
HARBIN, HEILONGJIANG PROVINCE, 2005

ALEXA BRUNET

Top

A ticket taker works from a booth outside a large boat sculpted in ice.
HARBIN, HEILONGJIANG PROVINCE, 2005

Bottom

Ice-sculpted buildings evoke Russia.
HARBIN, HEILONGJIANG PROVINCE, 2005

SAMUEL BOLLENDORFF
**Miners rehearse a show for
Christmas at the coal-mining town's
Protestant church.**
DATONG, SHANXI PROVINCE, 2006

Religion: The Chinese attitude toward religion can be described as casual. Not so long ago, a funeral could begin with masses said by Daoist (Taoist) and Buddhist priests in succession and, not impossibly, end with a Christian burial ceremony. The only common form of worship in China would be that of ancestors, but it is debatable whether it is a form of religion. Buddhists and Daoists co-existed (not always peacefully), and were tolerated and sometimes supported at every level of society. What religion never achieved in China was the status of a state religion. Not that Buddhists and Daoists didn't involve themselves in politics or interfered in affairs of state, it is rather that emperors and priests used each other for their own ends. With the revival of open religious worship in present-day China (with certain restrictions accorded to the Catholic Church—for historical and political reasons), the same indiscrimination can be observed. In the Lamaist temple, the Yonghe Gong, in Beijing, one of the most popular places of worship and tourism, where the visitor chokes with smoke from joss sticks, there is a chapel for the popular deity Guandi, the god of the military or Guardian of the North. There is a large population of Muslims in China, particularly in the northwest and south-west, and in Beijing. But Islam, in itself, has never been a problem in China. The complex situation in Xinjiang (Chinese Central Asia) where the native population is predominantly Muslim is again a matter of politics, national and international. **J. C. Y. W.**

Friday prayers at the Great Mosque
XINING, QINGHAI PROVINCE, 2005

153

**At a Daoist funeral, relatives carry the
casket to the family burial grounds.**
ZHEJIANG PROVINCE, 2003

MICHAEL WOLF
**The funeral offerings—a chicken,
a piece of pork, and a piece of
liver—symbolize three gods.**
ZHEJIANG PROVINCE, 2003

FRITZ HOFFMANN

Migrant workers celebrate their group wedding at a banquet with co-workers.
ZHONGSHAN, GUANGDONG PROVINCE, 2002

Family: The notion of an extended family of several generations living together under one roof (or, more accurately, within a large walled compound) may have been an ideal in the past, but was not often achieved—and only by a minority of prosperous households. On the other hand, people who were related usually managed to stay together in one place. There are still villages in China where all the inhabitants are kin to each other, bearing the same surname. Nearly every member of the parents' generation is an uncle or aunt. Thus the fear in some people's minds that the one-child policy will result in children growing up with no brother or sister is not entirely justified, or is at least premature. In the Chinese system, first cousins on the father's side, bearing the same surname, are brothers and sisters. There are still enough grandparents and parents who have brothers with children to provide brothers and sisters, uncles and aunts, even if they do not live together or in close proximity. Nevertheless, if the one-child rule continues to be strictly enforced, it will eventually transform the family structure in China; just how we do not yet know. Family relations in recent decades have been further eroded by mass movements of people, voluntary or involuntary. Urumqi in the far west, now teeming with Han Chinese from the interior provinces, was once a place of exile in the Qing dynasty. The difference today is that people are free to move back to where they came from after retirement or to change employment. Urban inhabitants go back to their home villages for festivals and celebrations. Holiday traffic in China is as heavy and as much a hardship as anywhere else, whether one moves by bus, train, bicycle, or, in very recent years, in one's own car. Families are holding together, so far. J. C. Y. W.

A stall sells pink plastic baby boys for fertility prayers at the tomb of Fuxi, mythic creator of the Chinese race.
HUAIYANG, HENAN PROVINCE, 2003

GILLES SABRIÉ
**Relatives and neighbors gather round
to admire a family's baby son.**
ANHUI PROVINCE, 2006

161

**The photographer's traditional
Chinese family included
several children.**
QUANGDONG PROVINCE, 2000

OLIVIER PIN-FAT

Top

Summoned home for his grandfather's funeral, the photographer arrives in his village.
QUANGDONG PROVINCE, 2000

Bottom

Family members light joss sticks.
QUANGDONG PROVINCE, 2000

OLIVIER PIN-FAT

The funeral ceremonies end with a banquet.
QUANGDONG PROVINCE, 2000

china: Working

Working: Never in the history of the world have so many lives been improved so much in such a short time.

Beginning in 1979 when Chinese leader Deng Xiaoping dismantled Maoist communes, divided state-owned farm-land into individual family plots, and allowed farmers to sell goods in open markets, China's economic growth has been on a rocket trajectory, one that gained further fuel in 1984 when Deng famously proclaimed "to get rich is glorious." What Deng did was not complicated. He merely gave the Chinese people permission to do what they do best: work night and day to get ahead. They took the ball and ran with it and are still running today.

It shouldn't be surprising that China went from stagnant communism to thriving capitalism almost overnight. After 2,000 years of imperial rule, China's political and social structure had rotted and collapsed. The country needed a revolution, communism was the global revolution of the moment, and Mao Zedong was its prophet. At first Mao harnessed the Chinese people's deep-seated ambition and diligence to rebuild the country using a Soviet state-economy model. Industrialization swept the country and its citizens were indoctrinated and motivated to get China back on its economic feet to catch up with the industrialized West using a better formula. The effort made considerable progress from 1949 until the late 1950s.

Then the growing rift with the Soviet Union prompted Mao to oust the 10,000 Soviet advisors resident in China and to resort to terror and psychological manipulation in the 20-year madness that came to be known as the Great Leap Forward and the Cultural Revolution. After tasting the fruits of progress, suddenly people were pitted against one another, ideology tramped practicality and the experiment ended in one of the world's most spectacular political, economic, and social catastrophes.

When Deng took over in 1978, the Chinese workforce was in a collective coma. Office workers slurped tea and read newspapers all day. Factory workers lazed around smoking and sleeping. Farmers worked just hard enough to ward off starvation and sneaked what they could from the commune food and financial reserves.

Then Deng offered the Chinese people their opportunity. He announced it in two steps, but he didn't have to say it twice. The people seized the chance and ran away with it, dragging the stumbling government behind like a ski boat dragging a water skier who has only minimal control over the boat's speed and course. The Chinese people are convinced that their country is destined to be great and is now emerging from a long slump. They aren't about to let it sink back behind the developed world.

Nature has not been kind to China. It has few natural resources. Oil, precious metals, and usable land are in short supply. But the country has one remarkable resource in abundance: millions of the world's most ambitious and hard-working people who, given the chance, focus intently on educating their children, compete ferociously with one another, and exercise a remarkable entrepreneurial mindset.

The result of this explosive release of pent-up ambitions has been one of the most astounding economic transformations in history. China chalks up 10 percent annual growth every year like clockwork. From 1978 to 2005, China increased its real gross domestic product 12-fold to become the world's fourth largest economy and third largest trader. At the same time, its manufacturing workforce more than doubled to more than 100 million people, and China has become the world's workshop. China's exports bring the country some $200 billion in additional foreign exchange reserves every year. The Chinese themselves are as parsimonious as they are industrious. As farmers gathered new cash income in the 1980s, and factory workers did so in the 1990s, they shoved their money into Chinese banks, giving the country an individual savings rate of nearly 50 percent.

The train stations are the place where one sees and feels the masses of China. Raw and ready peasants huddle under their bundles of clothing as they arrive to search for opportunity in Chinese cities. The sheer energy in the cities can be almost frightening. This is a workforce that lives in corrugated shacks, a dozen to a room, working seven days a week to bring money back to their families. They have built hundreds of new ports, airports, power plants, and dams; tens of thousands of apartment and office buildings; hundreds of thousands of miles of roads, highways, rail lines, and subways. China is and has been one huge construction project. Farm boys leave their families to become welders, bricklayers, cement finishers, and high-rise steel workers. Teenage boys carry baskets of coal on their backs, up and down mining shafts, for $1 per 12-hour day. Farm girls sew garments, assemble toys, connect circuit boards, clean fish, sort produce, serve food, separate garbage, and swaddle the infants of others while living in cramped dormitories where sleep, showers, and recreation are stolen moments from the production line.

At another level China's cities are all about speed, greed, and competition. China has the fastest elevator doors in the world. People get on elevators before others can get off. China is a place where a foreign executive can meet a Chinese worker by happenstance and then find him walking into his office every few weeks with business propositions. The Chinese Communist Party seems to realize that its only chance of staying in power is to maintain stability and keep everybody working and moving ahead as their expectations grow. That explains the exponential growth in education facilities. Between 1990 and 2004, China built some 700 new universities and enrollment tripled to more than than 4 million grads from 1.6 million grads. China has sent an estimated 600,000 students abroad to study and some 150,000 have returned. Many who don't come back permanently nevertheless shuttle back and forth to do business in their homeland. The country now has some 150 domestic MBA programs, several dozen of which are in conjunction with American and European universities.

China's rapid and successful economic development is now beginning to scare the rest of the world. At first it was factory workers in the developed world who looked at China and saw the looming loss of their jobs to laborers who earn $100 a month and often work seven days a week. But the competition now is going upscale. China is producing more than 800,000 engineering graduates per year. Tens of thousands of well-educated and highly motivated Chinese scientists and researchers are now working on stem cells, materials sciences, electronics, rocketry, satellites, software, silicon chips, and cyberspace experimentation at some 800 research-and-development centers operated by multinationals and thousands of others organized by the government or Chinese companies. Chinese financiers and investment bankers are top players in global capital markets and merger-and-acquisition activities.

But China is not the juggernaut that many believe. The Chinese economy is only one-fifth the size of America's. The country's largest and most prominent businesses are still state-owned and riddled with corruption and debilitating politics. Some 60 percent of Chinese exports come from foreign invested firms, and that percentage is closer to 80 percent for electronic and telecom products. Chinese brand names have failed to spread around the globe despite the government's effort to push 120 Chinese companies to become global brand names, and despite the fact that the government has mandated that 50 Chinese companies must become members of the Fortune 500 by 2010.

More important, though, are the tensions that are growing behind the scenes, both in the cities and in the countryside. At first glance, the timeless Chinese countryside seems tranquil. Farmers are planting rice, sowing grain, harvesting produce, and living with their pigs, ducks, and chickens as they have for millennia. But farm incomes have been stagnant since the first years of Deng's reforms. Farmers are surviving on remittances from children working in the cities. The Chinese countryside has some 450 million people of working age. Fewer than 200 million are needed on the country's postage-stamp-size farm plots.

The Chinese countryside is shifting from timeless to restless. Farm girls still marry into families where they become the virtual slaves of their mother-in-law. It's a particularly frustrating existence today when satellite television beams soap operas celebrating the glitz and glamour of Shanghai and the conspicuous wealth of a country that is producing the globe's largest stock market public offerings. The result has been an epidemic of female suicide in the countryside as girls who can't escape to work in cities give up and drink pesticide. Farmers are openly expressing resentment when once feared party officials come to take their land for a pittance to build luxury housing or industrial plants that disgorge toxic chemicals into their rural water supply. Riot police are as busy in the Chinese countryside today as are agricultural officials.

Mao's Cultural Revolution assaulted the Chinese family and social system. Children were forced to denounce parents, and students tortured and sometimes killed teachers for mostly imagined political mistakes. Deng's economic revolution is wreaking its own damage. Farm kids are growing up without their parents because migrant workers often leave their children behind with grandparents.

The mounting problems are more apparent in the cities. Buyers from Wal-Mart and other giant retail chains constantly squeeze factory margins to keep prices down. Migrant workers are exploited. They have little or no access to hospitals and health care. If their kids come with them, they are usually barred from attending local schools. They are second-class citizens in their own country.

In urban areas, only half of the people have health insurance. In rural areas, fewer than one-fifth are covered. The International Monetary Fund said that in 2005 only 14 percent of China's workforce was covered by unemployment insurance. China is also choking on its success. Two-thirds of energy in China comes from coal, most of it high sulfur. China is now number two in greenhouse gases behind the United states. The air is toxic in much of China, home to 16 of the world's 20 most polluted cities. China's rivers flow Technicolor with industrial effluents.

Amid it all, the population is anxious and stressed out. World-class restaurants, lavish spas, gyrating discos and nightclubs, plush suburban homes, and luxurious apartments litter the Chinese landscape that just yesterday was filled with people in Mao suits riding bicycles to collect their winter's allocation of cabbage. Despite this newfound prosperity, the people are empty inside. They compete, compete, compete, run after the next opportunity, and run over anybody who gets in their way. People want more money and higher and higher positions. The pace of life is relentless, that of a diligent student cramming for the next test and then striving to reach the next rung on the ladder. These high achievers are confident and prosperous on the outside, but all too often insecure and frightened on the inside. How those insecurities will play out over the long run is difficult to predict.

Perhaps China's most worrisome problem today, though, is one of its least discussed: the sustainability of this boom. The one-child policy instituted in 1979 is leading to a rapidly aging population and dwindling workforce to feed China's ravenous factories. Contrary to the popular notion, China does not have an endless supply of young peasants who will migrate to the cities to work in factories for low wages. Today there are some 110 million people in the Chinese countryside age 20–29, the prime factory working years. China's factory workforce has to be replenished every five or six years because most of these young workers head home with their nest eggs after that period of time spent in grueling factory work and cramped dorms. Just six years ago, there were 160 million people in the countryside age 20–29. By the year 2030, this number is projected to drop to below 50 million.

What are the implications? China will have a shortage of cheap labor. Wages will have to rise dramatically to keep workers in the factories, and factories will have to move inland to be closer to the workers' homes, thereby dramatically increasing transport costs. Already factory wages in some places in China have begun to rise 12 percent a year.

There is no question that the Chinese will keep working hard. Hard work is in their genes. But they will have to be better paid and better treated to do so. ∎

Agriculture: It is all about food in China. People usually don't drink alcohol without a meal in front of them, and they don't do any important business or socializing without a table groaning with delicacies that are often at the edge of their spending power. Many regions in China have their own distinct cuisine and specialties, from the hairy crabs of suburban Shanghai to the dumplings of Beijing to the hand-pulled noodles of Lanzhou to the goat cheese and ham of Yunnan to the rat, civet, owl, snake, cat menageries of culinary tastes of Guangdong. The majority of Chinese people live within eyesight or arm's reach of the beginnings of the food chain. A Chinese farmer lives with his animals and can grow anything anywhere, even if he has to hand feed water to shoots in a sand pit. Some 800 million of China's 1.3 billion live in the countryside, with comfortable farmers earning only the equivalent of several hundred U.S. dollars a year in cash income. They eat what they grow and raise. They sell pickled pigs face on the platforms of train stations, haul cabbage by donkey cart into Beijing, grow vast fields of flowers that would make Holland blush, and peddle fruit alongside every road in the country to increase their cash income. With a surplus of more than 200 million people of working age in the countryside who aren't needed on the farm, this *liu dong ren kou* or "roving population" crisscrosses China in search of any menial task that will create cash income. Any train station in China today looks like America's Ellis Island during the turn-of-the-century storm of immigration to America. China's internal immigration from the countryside to the city—at least 150 million in the past 20 years—has been the rocket fuel of the soaring export growth. China has always ridden to greatness or prosperity on the backs of the farmers, and it has been no different this time whether they stayed on the farm or became laborers in the cities. **J. McG.**

MICHAEL WOLF

A woman carries bags of rice in the traditional Chinese way.
FUJIAN PROVINCE, 2006

174

JULIA CALFEE

Kashi Market is the most important traditional market in Central Asia.
KASHI, XINJIANG,
UYGUR PROVINCE, 2005

**The newly built city of Fengdu
encroaches on the old town.**
FENGDU, CHONGQING, 2006

Fishermen lift their dip nets at dawn from the waters of the Yangzi River.
YIBIN, SICHUAN PROVINCE, 1998

181

**Young girls perform acrobatics on the
street to earn money.**
CHANGCHUN, JILIN PROVINCE, 2006

Street Work: Capitalism in China can often feel like a mugging. Walk down many city center streets where shops and restaurants draw crowds and you find yourself under assault. Young boys pull up their shirt sleeves to display a selection of glittering fake luxury watches. Others sidle up and flip open boxes, whispering "DVD DVD DVD look, look, movies and TV shows. Very cheap." Peasant beggars push at you, holding babies with dirt-smeared faces. Handicapped people thrust deformed limbs in your direction. Child acrobats and contortionists twist and turn and tangle themselves into knots to get your attention and a few coins. Teenage girls wearing tiny skirts and buckets of make-up stand in massage parlor doorways promising a good time. Sometimes it seems like everybody in China is on the make, all the time, day and night. But to be born a nobody in a population of 1.3 billion, in the middle of a frenetic gold-rush economy, motivates people to rush around to grab the next opportunity, and the next one, and the next one, and do just about anything to earn a buck. For the most part, there is a cheerfulness amid all this activity. Life is much better than it used to be, and it is going to get better in the future. As long as people have that attitude, China can move ahead. But 20 years of breakneck growth has built huge expectations in China. J. McG.

GILLES SABRIÉ

**Unemployed youths indicate their
skills in Chengdu's labor market.**
CHENGDU,
SICHUAN PROVINCE, 2003

186

SAMUEL BOLLENDORFF

A man and his son gather a few pieces of coal for their house.
TAIYUAN, SHANXI PROVINCE, 2006

Coal: The rocks have not been kind to China. The country has little crude oil and no great deposits of precious metals. What China does have is coal, seemingly endless seams of coal, most of it the high-sulfur variety that results in China being home to 16 of the world's 20 worst air-polluted cities. You can almost chew on the air in many Chinese cities, and coal has been the main culprit in an estimated 400,000 premature deaths a year from pollution-related respiratory diseases. Every ten days or so China opens up a new coal-fired power plant to satisfy the country's insatiable need for energy. People who once lived in brick huts now reside in modern apartment buildings with multiple air conditioners, entertainment centers, washing machines, microwaves, and an automobile in the garage below. Those who keep these luxuries humming are China's coal miners, the some 3.7 million peasant boys and grizzled men with blackened faces who have the deadliest job in China. Government statistics say that more than 250,000 coal miners have died in accidents in China since the PRC was founded in 1949, and that while producing 35 percent of the world's coal, China has some 80 percent of the world's coal mining deaths, with the official average being more than 6,000 miners a year. Additionally, some 600,000 Chinese coal miners are suffering from black lung, and this figure increases by some 70,000 miners a year. The problem is that tens of thousands of China's coal mines are small operations run by unscrupulous operators who are protected by corrupt local government officials. The government has a goal to close down 4,000 of these mines per year to save lives and reduce pollution. J. McG.

SAMUEL BOLLENDORFF

Top

Hao Laowu, a miner for 20 years, says, "They say we are 'the heroes of Chinese industry,' but they want our blood and our sweat."
TAIYUAN, SHANXI PROVINCE, 2006

IAN TEH

Bottom

Female workers at a coal mine outside Datong, the coal capital of China
DATONG, SHANXI PROVINCE, 2006

IAN TEH

Top

A view from a hotel window overlooking the polluted skyline of Datong
DATONG, SHANXI PROVINCE, 2006

Bottom

Children play in fields overlooking coal mining villages.
SHANXI PROVINCE, 2006

IAN TEH

**Miners return home after a shift
in the coal pits.**
SHANXI PROVINCE, 2006

GILLES SABRIÉ
**Workers at the Baotou Iron and Steel
Group, a state-owned enterprise**
BAOTOU, INNER MONGOLIA, 2006

**Construction of a subway system
in the Luohu area of Shenzhen**
SHENZHEN, GUANGDONG PROVINCE,
2002

TONY LAW
**A highway overpass in
the Panyu district**
GUANGZHOU, 2002

JOHN STANMEYER
**Laborers toil day and night carrying
dirt sucked up from the Yangzi River.**
CHONGQING, SICHUAN PROVINCE, 1999

Migrant Workers: They come from the farms to the cities with bundles of clothing, raw, ruddy, and ready to do anything to earn money to send home to relatives in their impoverished villages. Their opportunities are at the bottom of China's economic ladder, but that is better than staying on the family farm where cash incomes the equivalent of $100 or $200 a year are not uncommon. For salaries of up to several hundred dollars a month, they rub the feet and bodies of the wealthy in massage parlors; endure grinding 12-hour-days on assembly lines; feed, clothe, and nurture the children of the urban middle class; slog through mud digging tunnels; creep across the steel girders of skyscrapers under construction; carry golf bags; serve food and drink; and even cultivate suburban farm plots for urban peasants who now work in the cities and can't be bothered with farm work. They live in construction site tin shacks, 12-person dorm rooms where bunks are stacked like firewood, or on a cot laid out next to the washing machine of their employer's home. Their few leisure moments are often spent as voyeurs, wandering the streets peering into the doorways of glitzy nightclubs and fancy restaurants before sitting at street stalls sharing bowls of noodles and bottles of beer with friends. They flood home for Chinese New Year to display their new wealth and sophistication. But they return to the cities quickly because there is no cash to earn at home. **J. McG.**

GREG GIRARD

**Migrant workers leaving on the train
for jobs in Guangdong Province.**
CHANGSA, 1996

Migrant workers eat their lunch near the tracks they are working on.
SHANGHAI, 2005

A migrant worker cleans windows.
BEIJING, 2006

A farmer from Zhejiang now works as a scaffold erector on construction of one of Shanghai's new buildings.
SHANGHAI, 1997

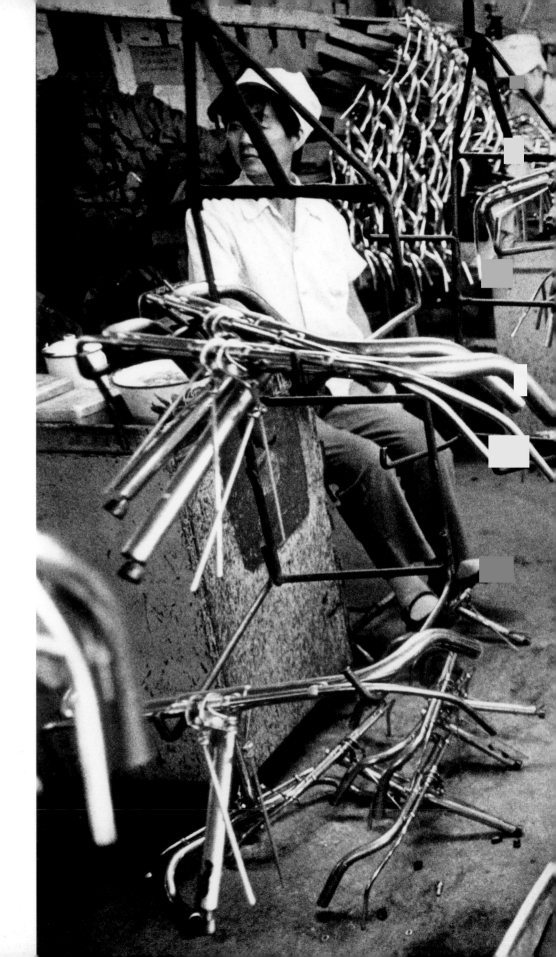

SEBASTIAO SALGADO

**Workers assemble handlebars
at the Forever Factory, a bicycle
assembly workshop.**
SHANGHAI, 1996

STEPHANE REMAEL
A worker's cubicle
BEIJING, 2006

MICHAEL WOLF
Opposite
Workers' living quarters
GUANGDONG PROVINCE, 2004

**A lack of success in the city prompted
this girl to return home.**
GUANGXI PROVINCE, 2004

STEPHANE REMAEL

Employees at the Chateau Maison Laffitte await potential clients, rich Chinese who can afford a meal in one of the hotel's private dining rooms.
BEIJING, 2007

NINA BERMAN

**Migrant workers take dance lessons
at a city park.**
SHENZHEN, GUANGDONG PROVINCE,
2004

**Manpower's Shanghai office specializes
in permanent job placement
and headhunting.**
PUDONG DISTRICT, SHANGHAI, 2006

The Center for Plant Transformation researches genetically modified plants, including rice and corn.
BEIJING, 2005

Hi-Tech: If you stand on the Bund riverfront of old Shanghai, in front of the granite edifices built by the Europeans and Americans in the 1800s when Shanghai was run by foreigners, one can see the shape of new Shanghai, a district known as Pudong. The space-age skyline of futuristic high-rises looks like it was drawn by the illustrators of the *Jetsons* cartoon show. And Pudong is not alone. The country that is furiously rebuilding its place in the world through low-cost labor and exports of garments, toys, shoes, and knick-knacks of every sort has been simultaneously moving up the technology chain. Multinationals have created more than a thousand research and development centers in China, which will make China a central player in the world's innovation chain as it now is in the world's supply chain for consumer products. China is aggressively working to lure home researchers and inventors who were among the nearly 600,000 to head overseas to study in the past 25 years. And government money is being generously allocated to labs aimed at making China a world leader in everything from materials science to biotechnology to silicon chips to aerospace. The underlying question is whether a government that controls information, limits free speech, and indoctrinates as it educates can produce the talent and scientific ecosystem for innovation. For now, the country is leading at "incremental innovation," taking the intellectual property and inventions of others and refining ever better commercial products. **J. McG.**

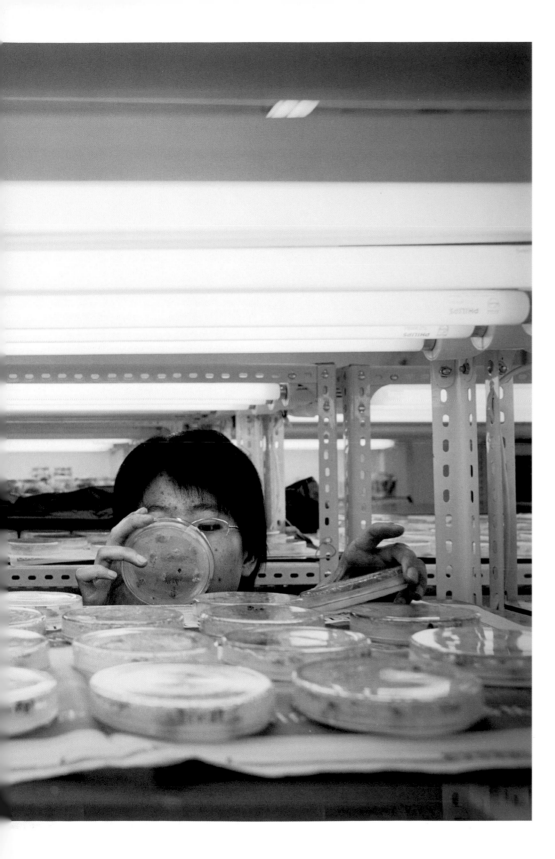

QILAI SHEN
Top

Factory workers assemble automobiles at the Shanghai Volkswagen (SVW) plant.
SHANGHAI, 2006

ALESSANDRO DIGAETANO
Bottom

Dalian is China's biggest crude oil terminal.
DALIAN, LIAONING PROVINCE, 2004

Hong Kong's International Terminal is the world's largest container port.
HONG KONG, 1997

ALESSANDRO DIGAETANO

The Beijing National Stadium, dubbed the "bird's nest," was built to host the 2008 Summer Olympic Games.
BEIJING, 2006

china: Modernization

Modernization:

No images or words can adequately capture the magnitude of economic modernization and social change under way in China in the past three decades. Even statistics, favored measurements of the revolutionary transformation of the Middle Kingdom, barely convey the unprecedented material progress China has made since the East Asian giant awakened from the nightmare of the Cultural Revolution in 1976. In the 30 years since the country abandoned radical communism, per capita income has increased 12 times, more than 150 million peasants have migrated to the cities, and an estimated 400 million have been lifted out of abject poverty. The improvement in the standard of living for the average Chinese has been so rapid that, within one generation, the same people who subsisted on about 2,000 calories per person a day 30 years ago are now fighting an epidemic of obesity.

Economic growth and the opening to the outside world, the twin engines hurtling China toward modernity, have expanded individual freedoms and choices beyond the wildest dreams of those who can still remember the day the late dictator Mao Zedong died (September 9, 1976). Under Mao, the country was sealed off to the outside world; listening to the BBC or the VOA was a crime punishable by long jail terms; travel to the West was simply unheard of; owning a private telephone was the privilege of the ruling elite; as for fashion, to paraphrase Henry Ford, Chinese people could wear anything they wanted, as long as it was a dark-blue Mao jacket. Fast forward to 2006. China today boasts the world's largest telephone network (with 800 million cell-phone and fixed-line subscribers); 140 million Chinese surf the Internet;

half a million Chinese students have gone to the West to pursue higher education, and 32 million Chinese traveled abroad on business and for pleasure in 2006. No Chinese official would be caught dead wearing a drab Mao jacket today; their preferred attire is Gucci or Armani.

China is also in the midst of a new cultural revolution. Despite persistent, albeit erratic, government controls, Chinese arts, movies, television entertainment, and literature have experienced a renaissance. Within China, they have replaced the revolutionary songs and operas that were the only entertainment available for the masses during the Mao era. On the global stage, Chinese films, such as *Farewell My Concubine, Raise the Red Lantern, To Live,* and *Beijing Bicycle,* have won rave reviews from critics abroad and give Western moviegoers an opportunity to experience the newfound cultural freedom of the Chinese people. Chinese artists, once limited to glorifying socialism, are now displaying their bold experimental works in Paris and New York—and fetching prices undreamed by their predecessors.

Of course, cultural exchange is a two-way street. The impact of Western culture, including cultural imports from China's immediate neighbors, has been profound within China. American sci-fi series, South Korean historical drama, fashion shows in Milan, the Academy Awards, and NBA games are among the most watched TV programs in China. On the streets of Shanghai and Beijing, bootlegged copies of the latest Hollywood movies are available for the equivalent of a dollar (although the subtitles are so ineptly translated that one wonders whether their Chinese customers can get the real story).

Preceding Pages
Zhang Xiaogang, one of China's best-known artists, works in his studio.
BEIJING, 2007

Even Western rock, once condemned as the epitome of capitalist decadence, has conquered a sizeable young population in China. One can only imagine what Mao is doing in his grave.

The physical transformation of China is nothing short of breathtaking. Thirty years ago, China had no expressway and only a handful of high-rises. The dominant mode of urban transportation was bicycle. Today, it has the world's second largest network of superhighways. Chinese metropolises look indistinguishable from those in the West: Cars clog the streets, neon signs light up the night, and gleaming tall buildings dominate the skylines. But the Middle Kingdom's rush to prosperity has barely begun. Factories, ports, power plants, railways, the sinews of a modern economy, are springing up so fast that, according to one estimate, China is adding the equivalent of a greater Philadelphia each year.

No one, including the most starry-eyed optimists, could have foreseen China's new great leap forward in the last 30 years. Deng Xiaoping, the man most responsible for igniting Beijing's modernization drive, would certainly have been proud. He would not be alone feeling giddy about China's success and its bright prospects. According to many polls, the Chinese people are among the most optimistic in the world today. The obsession of the Chinese, especially the younger generation, is no longer how to carry out Mao's class struggle, but how to keep winning in the marketplace of global capitalism.

The future, it seems, belongs to China.

Does it?

If you take the breathless media coverage of a rising China at its face value, you will definitely miss the dark side of China's frenzied quest for modernization. For all its achievements since the late 1970s, China still has a long way to go in realizing its age-old collective ambition of becoming a truly strong and prosperous nation. Today, despite scoring double-digit growth year after year, China remains a developing country with a per capita income of $2,000 (one-20th of the U.S. level). More than 40 percent of the population, mostly residents in remote desolate villages, still live on less than two dollars a day and have yet to enjoy the full benefits of China's new-found prosperity. Largely hidden from main tourist attractions and booming cities, this group lacks access to clean drinking water and basic health care. Any accident—sickness, natural disaster, or some other misfortune—could plunge them into misery.

More worrisome, modernization is generating new tensions and strains that are tearing apart China's social fabric. Instead of wiping out regional and urban-rural disparities, China's economic take-off has exacerbated them, especially since the 1990s. At the early stages of the reform in the 1980s, balanced development strategies spread the fruits of economic growth more evenly. But in the last decade and a half, a combination of government policy (preference for capital-intensive fixed investment, neglect of agriculture, and underinvestment in social services), industrial restructuring, higher rewards for professionals and entrepreneurs, and concentration of economic development along the coast has widened the coastal-interior, urban-rural, and rich-poor gaps. Today, the income of a typical urban resident, including government subsidies in health care, housing, and education, is six times that of a rural resident—no other country in the world has as wide a urban-rural income gap. Even in urban areas, more than 20 million residents, mainly the unemployed and disabled, have fallen into poverty. Income inequality in China, extremely low in the late 1970s, is approaching Latin American levels.

Inevitably, the Chinese themselves are wondering: We may be getting rich gloriously, but are we creating a just society?

Those worried about where China is headed do not have to look far to find disturbing signs of growing social inequities and injustices. Why has China, they ask, built the world's most expensive Formula One racing course but provides health insurance only to 10 percent of its population? How come China has wasted tens of billions of yuan in projects that burnish the image of local officials but chosen not to make free primary education available to all? Why do local governments keep grabbing land from millions of poor peasants to erect fancier shopping malls and polluting factories? (Today, the number of landless peasants has exceeded 40 million—more than the entire population of Poland.) What exactly, by the way, is a replica of the Palace of Versailles, home to a tycoon, doing in Changsha, a stone's throw from Mao's birthplace? Why has China become Bentley's biggest market, where newly minted billionaires snapped up 70 of the 200 ultra-luxury cars, at $250,000 apiece, sold worldwide in 2003? How can one reconcile this with heartbreaking stories of farmers committing suicide because they could not afford to pay their children's tuitions?

What, in one word, has happened to China?

These questions encapsulate the many Chinas that are being simultaneously destroyed and created in the country's time-compressed dash toward modernity. Unquestionably, the Maoist China demolished by Deng's economic revolution was a totalitarian nightmare. No one should shed any tears for its demise. But the creation of a new China has produced such social dislocation, stress, and popular disillusionment that many people have grown nostalgic for the Mao era. The portraits of the late dictator, who was directly responsible for the worst famine in human history, have resurfaced. Many restaurants serve dishes touted as "Chairman Mao's favorites" (the most popular of which is extra fatty pork, stewed in soy sauce). Of course, one can detect crude commercial motives in exploiting the lingering mystique of the late tyrant; after all, in a country where the respect for intellectual property rights is less than perfect, protecting the Mao brand is impossible. Yet, the growing appeal of Maoist leftism, not just among a small band of intellectuals, cannot be dismissed as a mere transitory aberration.

Indeed, social discontent has found fertile soil and even violent expressions in today's China. On any given day, there are more than 200 riots and collective protests involving an average of 50 people each. Crime is soaring. Anti-rich rhetoric has become fashionable because most Chinese believe that the wealthy have gotten rich through corruption. Even though such scattered incidents of social unrest and incipient leftist populism have not precipitated a national political upheaval, they are symptoms of a deeper political malaise that the Chinese leadership has chosen not to confront. Most of the ruling elites are convinced that all this is just "growing pains."

However, if China maintains its current strategy of "modernization at any cost," the question becomes whether the cost is sustainable—not just politically, as the social costs of such a strategy become too much for the population to bear, but also economically, as the accumulated social neglect, political strains, and environmental degradation drain the country's dynamism and slow down its modernization.

This pessimistic scenario may recall the tragic failure of China's first-generation modernizers—the mandarins of the late Qing dynasty. More than a century ago, they stuck to the dogma of *zhongxue weiti xixue weiyong* (translated as "Chinese learning as essence; Western learning for practical use") and failed to see the connection between economic modernization and the institutional and cultural underpinnings of Western civilization. Early Chinese modernizers believed that all they needed to do to make China modern was to acquire the West's technologies without importing its institutions, values, or political systems. History proved them disastrously wrong.

Today, China's new modernizers appear to be repeating history, albeit on an even more gigantic scale. Intriguingly, the dominant mindset of China's ruling elite today is remarkably similar to that of the late Qing period. As long as China can deliver double-digit growth and maintain its economic modernization on course, the thinking in Beijing goes, all the other problems will be solved. Indeed, proponents of this view insist that only a dominant state and a one-party system can mobilize resources, set national priorities, and keep social order. China does not need political modernization (a.k.a. democratic reform) to succeed. As the late Deng Xiaoping, perhaps one of the greatest modernizers in history, warned, introducing democracy and multiparty politics would bring chaos, and modernization would grind to a halt.

China's amazing economic progress since 1978, achieved under one-party rule, seems to vindicate this authoritarian doctrine. Unfortunately, this deceptively appealing theory may have outlived its usefulness. True, the Chinese government should be justifiably proud of its record in promoting market reforms, attracting foreign investment, and alleviating poverty. But its resistance to political reforms—introducing the rule of law, empowering an increasingly pluralist society, and making government officials responsive and accountable to the public—is exacerbating many of the social ills now afflicting China. As long as local officials are rewarded for building "hardware"—roads, factories, and shopping centers—at the expense of social investments, public health, education, and the environment will suffer. In the absence of greater press freedom and a vibrant civil society, official corruption and abuses of power cannot be contained.

Fortunately, Chinese leaders are not blind to the mounting social tensions—judging by their call for a Confucian "harmonious society" and recent reforms aimed at improving the lives of the country's most disadvantaged. However, it remains unclear whether they are ready to embrace the more difficult and dangerous challenge of political reform.

So here we are: marveling at the spectacular economic and social progress achieved by the Chinese people in the past three decades, but feeling uncertain about where their government is leading them next. Let us hope that a combination of good luck and better leadership will help China overcome the daunting odds ahead—inequality, environmental decay, financial turmoil, and brewing social dissatisfaction. The world's stakes in China—a nuclear power and the world's fourth largest economy—are far greater today than a century ago. A China succeeding in modernization is no threat to global peace and prosperity. A failing China is. ■

A dinner party at G's Club for
the opening of Contrasts Gallery
SHANGHAI, 2007

SAMUEL BOLLENDORFF
**The new Pudong business district
seen from the Jin Mao Tower**
SHANGHAI, 2007

CHARLES OMMANNEY

A Chinese Michael Jackson look-alike poses for visitors in Tiananmen Square.
BEIJING, 2006

KEVIN LEE

Top

Souvenirs with Mao's portrait are for sale in sites popular with tourists.
BEIJING, 2001

GILLES SABRIÉ

Bottom

Among the working class, Mao is still revered; whatever wrongdoing is blamed on his entourage.
BEIJING, 2003

JODI COBB
Top

A giant poster of Mao Zedung hangs at the Gate of Heavenly Peace, one of the entrances to the Forbidden City.
BEIJING, 1981

MICHAEL S. YAMASHITA
Bottom

Political posters with Mao Zedong slogans hang on the walls of the Party headquarters.
ZHOUCHENG, YUNNAN PROVINCE, 1991

233

Store workers fix a mirror on a busy commercial street.
BAOTOU, INNER MONGOLIA, 2006

Provinces in Transition: The tide of modernization and consumerism has reached—and is transforming—China's interior. By most accounts, the less developed inland provinces are still way behind the coastal regions in fashion, leisure, entertainment, and consumption. But they are catching up fast—thanks to rising standards of living, the spread of television, foreign cultural influence, and irrepressible private entrepreneurship. Since the early 1990s, market liberalization and massive improvements in physical and telecommunications infrastructure have enabled these previously isolated and impoverished regions to prosper as well. The effects on the quality of life of the average individual in these areas are revolutionary. Previously, few of them could afford decent consumer goods or travel, let alone luxuries such as color television sets or private automobiles. Today, they not only own the usual household appliances, but also aspire to enjoy the same lifestyle as their fellow countrymen along the coast. The younger generation has set their sights even higher. For them, the influence of Western culture, ranging from pop songs to movies, and sports, is simply too cool to resist. Yet, the historical, cultural, and political legacies of the past have not been wiped out. In these areas, the old and new, the static and the dynamic, co-exist uneasily. M. P.

**A chair occupies a green space with
a view of a satellite city.**
HONG KONG, 2003

MICHAEL WOLF
Dressed in their finest fake leather, two girls come home to their village for New Year's.
FUJIAN PROVINCE, 2003

Old men congregate in one of the water towns west of Shanghai.
WUHZEN, ZHEJIANG PROVINCE, 2006

ALEX MAJOLI
A woman offers massage.
SHENZHEN, GUANGDONG PROVINCE, 2003

Rich and Poor: Although it is common for fast-growing societies to experience rising income inequality, the rapidity of the increase in the income gap between the haves and the have-nots in China since the 1980s has been unprecedented. Most estimates suggest that income inequality has grown 50 percent in the past 30 years. Inevitably, such growing disparity has become highly visible and socially divisive. The newly rich flaunt their wealth by conspicuous consumption—driving fancy cars, wearing expensive Italian suits, and living in luxurious mansions. At the same time, the poor have suffered, albeit in relative terms. China's social safety net, never generous, has deteriorated even further. Wage income for the unskilled migrants, manual laborers, and laid-off factory workers has either stagnated or declined, while earnings for the professionals, government officials, and workers in state-controlled monopolies have risen substantially. Although China mints billionaires faster than most other countries, its ability to cut the poverty roll has not improved since the late 1980s. Yet, the Chinese government has maintained public policies that have only exacerbated the trends of inequality. Beijing levies no capital gains or inheritance taxes on the rich, but makes the poor pay for their health care and education. Not surprisingly, inequality has now become the most sensitive political issue in China. M. P.

FRITZ HOFFMANN

**Wang Bin is protesting the
government's refusal to pay for a
comparable replacement for his plot.**
DALIAN, LIAONING PROVINCE, 2005

**Mr. Lee, interior decorator and owner
of Classical Furniture, sits on a
reproduction French Empire sofa.**
BEIJING, 2005

PATRICK ZACHMANN

An elderly couple, who have lived in their traditional *hutong* (alley house) for 30 years, await displacement.
BEIJING, 2004

Displacement: When the People's Republic of China was founded in 1949, Chairman Mao Zedong declared that the country was a blank sheet of paper on which a new picture could be freely painted. But that was poetic hyperbole, at best. Of course, Mao ruled as if China were a blank sheet of paper, and the consequences were calamitous. Today, Chinese society is in the midst of an economic revolution that, though less deadly, is no less disruptive than Mao's class struggle. Commercial development is, literally, devouring entire neighborhoods and dismantling long-established communities. Very often, urban residents are forcibly moved out of their homes to make away for new real estate development. In some cases, local government officials even hire thugs to brutalize and evict residents who refuse to "sell" their homes at below-market prices. Undoubtedly, the booming real estate sector and urban development have made a small number of well-connected tycoons incredibly wealthy, at the expense of many voiceless ordinary citizens. Western visitors who admire the glistening highrises in Chinese cities are often unaware of the immeasurable human toll raw capitalism has exacted on Chinese society. **M. P.**

**The couple prepares a meal in their
old house in the center of Beijing.**
BEIJING, 2004

PATRICK ZACHMANN

Top
Their pet birds have moved into a new flat with them.
BEIJING, 2004

Bottom
The couple have been moved to the Zhaogongkou district, near the 4th ring road.
BEIJING, 2004

JULIA CALFEE

**A couple celebrates their marriage
at the Chateau Laffitte, a luxury hotel.**
BEIJING, 2005

Privilege: For those who have prospered in China's transitional economy, such as private entrepreneurs, professionals, and government officials, life can be very good. Access to consumer goods, even expensive imports, is now widely available to those willing and able to pay. The notorious system of rationing has become a distant memory. But rising prosperity and consumerism are creating incongruous cultural scenes throughout China. Some cultural imports—hairstyles, fashion, or architecture—appear to blend in poorly with local customs or scenes. Such concerns are obviously superfluous to those who are thoroughly enjoying their new-found freedoms, opportunities, and material success. For the older generation, perhaps the memories of the horrific deprivation under the radical rule of Maoism are so powerful that any pleading for self-restraint in face of the onslaught of materialism is futile. The younger generation, to whom "Cultural Revolution" or the "Great Leap Forward" are unfamiliar terms, appears to have taken a good life for granted. Who could blame them? Steeped in social Darwinism, as many of them are, China's privileged firmly believe they have earned their dues. **M. P.**

At Beijing Bokai Intelligence and Capability Kindergarten, parents see competence in golf as a step up in their children's networking skills.
BEIJING, 2004

MARK LEONG

A 14-year-old boy is treated at the Aimin Fat Reduction Hospital.
BEIJING, 2004

DAVID BUTOW

An "X games" demonstration and contest is held in a park in the north side of the city.
SHANGHAI, 2006

FRITZ HOFFMANN

**At the Vogue nightclub, a singer
entertains while a bargirl in the
members-only lounge awaits clientele.**
SHANGHAI, 2001

Pop Culture: It has often been said that, after the crackdown on the pro-democracy movement in Tiananmen in 1989, the Chinese government reached an unspoken "contract" with the Chinese people: So long as they do not challenge the authority of the Communist Party, the government would allow them to have unprecedented personal freedom in making money and experimenting with new lifestyles. Obviously, there is no way to verify whether such a bargain was ever struck. But on the surface, the government appears to have honored the "contract." Personal freedom, not political rights, is certainly flourishing throughout China. Western movies, music, arts, and entertainment, once labeled "spiritual pollution" in the early 1980s, are now widely available and highly popular. Indeed, many Chinese openly worry that Western, especially American, pop culture is destroying China's own rich traditional cultural heritage. It may take another half century for China as a whole to catch up with the West. But as consumers and pop culture fans, China's younger generation is almost indistinguishable from their Western counterparts. This is all to the good. However, one does wonder whether those who have taken personal freedom for granted will one day demand real political rights. M. P.

STEPHANE REMAEL
**Rich clients arrive at a nightclub
called MIX in the Chaoyang district.**
BEIJING, 2006

MATIAS COSTAS

A young woman tries make-up at a beauty center in a mall in the commercial district.
BEIJING, 2006

MARK LEONG

The showroom at Heyu Shoe Materials Co. displays soles and heels for sale to domestic and overseas companies.
WENZHOU, ZHEJIANG PROVINCE, 2006

NINA BERMAN

**A young hipster wearing a Dolce &
Gabbana outfit leaves a fashion show.**
BEIJING, 2006

MARK LEONG

**One of Beijing's biggest netbars,
520 Virtual Game World has about
350 terminals.**
BEIJING, 2004

MARK LEONG
A drive-in movie theater audience watches "The Lord of the Rings: The Return of the King."
BEIJING, 2006

SAMUEL BOLLENDORFF

Two young girls pass a billboard in front of a construction site.
BEIJING, 2006

GILLES SABRIÉ

Chairman Mao's face is reflected in the glass cover of a display of his notebook. Tourists can visit his parents' house.
CHANGSHA, HUNAN PROVINCE, 2006

PHOTOGRAPHY CREDITS

ABOUT THE AUTHORS

JONATHAN SPENCE is Sterling Professor of History at Yale University. He teaches in the field of Chinese history from around 1600 to the present, and on Western images of China since the Middle Ages. His books include *The Death of Woman Wang* (1978); *The Memory Palace of Matteo Ricci* (1984); *The Question of Hu* (1987); *Chinese Roundabout: Essays on History and Culture; The Gate of Heavenly Peace: The Chinese and their Revolution 1895–1980; The Chan's Great Continent: China in Western Minds*; and *God's Chinese Son* (1994). His research often takes him to many Chinese universities.

ELIZABETH ECONOMY is C.V. Starr Senior Fellow and Director of Asia Studies at the Council on Foreign Relations. Her most recent book, *The River Runs Black: The Environmental Challenge to China's Future,* won the 2005 International Convention on Asia Scholars award for best social sciences book. Her writings appear often in publications such as *Foreign Affairs, The New York Times, The Washington Post,* and *the International Herald Tribune,* and she is a frequent radio and television commentator on U.S.-China Relations.

JOSEPH FEWSMITH is Professor of International Relations and Political Science at Boston University, where he is also Director of the East Asian Interdisciplinary Studies Program. He is author of *Party, State and Local Elites in Republican China: Merchant Organizations and Politics in Shanghai, 1890–1930* (1985); *Dilemmas of Reform in China: Political Conflict and Economic Debate* (1994); *Elite Politics in Contemporary China* (2001); and *China Since Tiananmen: The Politics of Transition* (2001). He has written extensively on contemporary politics in China.

JAMES C. Y. WATT is Brooke Russell Astor Chairman of the Department of Asian Art at the Metropolitan Museum of Art. Mr. Watt began his career with the Metropolitan in 1985 as Senior Consultant for Chinese Antiquities and Decorative Arts. Mr. Watt has organized and contributed to the catalogues of a number of exhibitions at The Metropolitan Museum of Art, notable among them: "East Asian Lacquer" (1991), "Splendors of Imperial China" (with Wen C. Fong, 1996), "When Silk Was Gold" (with Anne Wardwell, 1998), "China: Dawn of a Golden Age, 200–750 AD" (2004), and "Defining Yongle: Imperial Art in the Early Fifteenth-Century China" (with Denise P. Leidy, 2005).

JAMES MCGREGOR is the chairman and CEO of JL McGregor & Company LLC, a research and advisory firm focused on China. A Mandarin speaker, he is a journalist-turned-businessman who has lived in China for 20 years and the author of the book *One Billion Customers: Lessons From the Front Lines of Doing Business in China.* From 1987 to 1993 McGregor served as *The Wall Street Journal*'s Taiwan bureau chief and *The Wall Street Journal*'s China bureau chief from 1993 to 2000. McGregor is currently a member of the National Committee on U.S.-China Relations; a member of the International Council of the Asia Society; and he serves on a variety of China-related advisory boards.

MINXIN PEI is a senior associate and the director of the China Program at the Carnegie Endowment for International Peace. He is the author of *China's Trapped Transition: The Limits of Developmental Autocracy* (2006) and *From Reform to Revolution: The Demise of Communism in China and the Soviet Union* (1994).

inside China

Published by the National Geographic Society

John M. Fahey, Jr., President and Chief Executive Officer

Gilbert M. Grosvenor, Chairman of the Board

Nina D. Hoffman, Executive Vice President;
   President, Book Publishing Group

Prepared by the Book Division

Kevin Mulroy, Senior Vice President and Publisher

Leah Bendavid-Val, Director of Photography
   Publishing and Illustrations

Marianne R. Koszorus, Director of Design

Barbara Brownell Grogan, Executive Editor

Elizabeth Newhouse, Director of Travel Publishing

Carl Mehler, Director of Maps

Staff for This Book

Rebecca Lescaze, Editor

Jane Menyawi, Illustrations Editor

Cinda Rose, Art Director

William Christmas III, Nicholas P. Rosenbach,
   Gregory Ugiansky, Map Research and Production

Clayton R. Burneston, Supervisor, Pre-Press

Richard S. Wain, Production Project Manager

Rob Waymouth, Illustrations Specialist

Cameron Zotter, Design Assistant

Jennifer A. Thornton, Managing Editor

Gary Colbert, Production Director

Manufacturing and Quality Management

Christopher A. Liedel, Chief Financial Officer

Phillip L. Schlosser, Vice President

John T. Dunn, Technical Director

Chris Brown, Director

Maryclare Tracy, Manager

Nicole Elliott, Manager

Founded in 1888, the National Geographic Society is one of the largest nonprofit scientific and educational organizations in the world. It reaches more than 285 million people worldwide each month through its official journal, NATIONAL GEOGRAPHIC, and its four other magazines; the National Geographic Channel; television documentaries; radio programs; films; books; videos and DVDs; maps; and interactive media. National Geographic has funded more than 8,000 scientific research projects and supports an education program combating geographic illiteracy.

For more information, please call
1-800-NGS LINE (647-5463)
or write to the following address:

National Geographic Society
1145 17th Street N.W.
Washington, D.C. 20036-4688 U.S.A.

Visit us online at
www.nationalgeographic.com/books

For information about special discounts
for bulk purchases, please contact
National Geographic Books Special Sales:
ngspecsales@ngs.org